Catalysts
Thoughts on Design Research for Meaningful Change

Edited by Nina Stegeman & Geke van Dijk / STBY

In collaboration with partners from the Reach Network for Global Design Research

Catalysts: Thoughts on Design Research for Meaningful Change
Edited by Nina Stegeman and Geke van Dijk (STBY)

Contributors: Aditya Prakash, Ayush Chauhan, Babitha George & Romit Ray (Quicksand, India), Bas Raijmakers (STBY, UK & Netherlands), Cal Bruns & Kelvin Kaari (Matchboxology, South Africa), Camila Boga & Kleber Puchaski (Flutter Innovation, Brazil), Chin Chin Burkolter & Kevin Tan (Somia CX (Indonesia & Singapore), Chris Marmo (Paper Giant, Australia), Daniel Szuc & Jo Wong (Apogee, Hong Kong), José de la O (delaO design studio, Mexico), Lekshmy Parameswaran & Laszlo Herczeg (The Care Lab, Spain), Marc Rettig (Fit Associates, US), Michael Davis-Burchatt (Big Human, Canada), Nicolas Gaudron & Virginia Cruz (IDSL, France), Rikke Ulk (Antropologerne, Denmark), Slava Kozlov & Katerina Khomenchuk (Summ( )n Futures, Russia & Netherlands), Yuki Uchida (Re:public, Japan).

Designed by Hyperkit
Printed by Swallowtail
Edition of 1000

Published by STBY Ltd.
De Beauvoir Block, Unit 5
92-96 De Beauvoir Road
London N1 4EN
United Kingdom
www.stby.eu
info@stby.eu

ISBN: 978-1-3999-1772-8

..STBY...

Preface

Creatives, designers and researchers often find themselves in the role of 'Catalysts' in complex change processes. This might be in projects commissioned by clients or partners or in self-initiated projects. Many of us identify ourselves as activists and ambassadors for system change.

The articles in this publication are particularly interested in creative contributions to 'Meaningful Change'. So not just in any change, as in change-for-change's-sake, but in meaningful change that makes a real difference to the everyday lives of people, organisations and the planet as a whole. We often feel as much like activists as professionals. Together with our clients and partners we have the opportunity to be catalysts for positive change through our work. And that element of meaningful activism and catalysation is in fact in many cases why our clients, partners and other stakeholders are choosing to work with us, and we with them.

Purpose, process and skill are strongly related. They naturally feed into each other. Purpose is what keeps us going in the right direction, while process and skill enable us to progress. However, in publications and conferences how we achieve our purpose often gets most of the attention. There are countless books, sites and courses about tools and methods and guidelines, while there are far less resources about the underlying intent of the work.

So that is the challenge we set ourselves with this publication. What are the implicit narratives that would benefit from some more explicit musing, and what do we as catalysts for positive change feel that the most urgent topics and emerging practices are? The range of articles in this publication reflects the result of that questioning. We have tried to reflect on the water we swim in, rather than the types of fish we are and see around us.

The co-authors of the various essays in this publication are all partners in the Reach Network. A global network of agencies specialised in human-centred design research and service innovation, working with businesses and non-profit organisations around the world. With this publication, we provide an inside look at how research and design practices are contributing to meaningful and positive change around the world. And in ways that the various partners from the Reach Network are expanding that mandate.

This publication shares examples and considerations about pluralistic travels in design and research adventures. Which says a lot about how the work of preparing the world for change is itself subject to change. Each themed section starts with a brief introduction on its specific angle to meaningful change, followed by an essay co-authored by a few partners from the Reach Network, and complemented by contributions from other partners around the world.

The essays in the publication do not represent a monocultural view. Nor do they agree on a specific notion of design or research. They rather offer a surprisingly wide range of observations on the various ways that design and research are contributing to many different meaningful change processes. We hope that the contents resonate with a wide range of research and design activists all over the globe.

See page 83–88 for more details on the Reach Network and the individual authors.

Many Ways to Meaningful Change (Reach Network conference, GOOD19)

"I can't understand why people are frightened of new ideas. I'm frightened of the old ones."

John Cage

Contents

In this section we examine an everyday occurrence, the end of life, and imagine why particular circumstances play out. What seems like a dark subject on the surface reveals so much about the things people strive for in a life well lived. As well as the meaning and therapeutic effects of designing for the end of life.

Death can be approached as a 'space' in which others can be invited. Design researchers seem to be suitable hosts for inviting people to enter the space of dying. They can help to designate a moment in time for people to encounter the space of death and open up the experience of dying at both an individual level, and as an engagement of a wider community.

The study of death reveals cultural boundaries where painful misunderstandings of tradition appear. Rather than waiting for news of an imminent death, or needing to have a traumatic, poor experience of managing the estate of a loved one for example, it is important to design ways to prompt proactive, sensitive, informed and meaningful conversations between individuals and their loved ones.

By approaching death as a space, designers have the opportunity to help people enter it and to explore. Conversation about death is a key strategy for inviting people to enter the space of dying and find out what is truly important while being alive.

Death is a Space

By Chris Marmo (Paper Giant, Australia) and Lekshmy Parameswaran & Laszlo Herczeg (The Care Lab, Spain)

"We are imperfect mortal beings, aware of that mortality even as we push it away, failed by our very complication, so wired that when we mourn our losses we also mourn, for better or for worse, ourselves. As we were. As we are no longer. As we will one day not be at all." Joan Didion, The Year of Magical Thinking

As we prepared the first draft of this chapter the pandemic struck, and our initial planning for discussing death as an object of design seemed shallow and incomplete without considering the impact of COVID-19 on communities the world over; people were dying alone and families were grieving apart, making the topic ever more relevant, but also more sensitive to discuss. As the year played out, our understanding of this moment solidified, and — multiple iterations later — we hope we've produced a chapter, and some conceptual tools, for others to make their own sense of this shared global experience of death and dying.

Death is a complex and taboo topic, and through it's medicalisation and professionalisation, has increasingly become an object of design — that is, a *problem to solve* through design. Human-centred design (HCD) naturally places humans at the centre of things. It's default is to try to understand the person, their traits and experiences, and 'pain points', and solve for them. Fundamentally, HCD focuses on '*humans with needs*', that is, on individuals whose needs are seen as innate, internal states that can be either delighted or disappointed.

Through our experience across multiple projects focused on the topic of death and dying, through which we've been asked to design better cemeteries, reimagine care homes and improve government services, we have found the concept of 'death' or 'dying' as an

internal state of a 'user' to be lacking. In addition, we've found the natural focus of HCD to hone in on the needs of the *individual* is limiting.

Taking into account the communal, shared nature of death which is experienced by a complex, ever-changing combination of a dying individual, loved ones and professionals, we want to propose a new way of thinking about death as an object of design. Rather than thinking of death as an *attribute* of an individual, or as a medical condition to be managed, it's more productive to think of it as an actor on the relationships *between* people. It is a thing that has its own *agency*; we can view it as a force that repels, attracts, prompts or stiffles conversations, changes behaviours and shifts intentions. It's something that either envelops or isolates, pushes or pulls people to as well as from it.

To help think through death as an object of design, we encourage you to think about it as something that exists in the world, outside of people. For this purpose, Death can be thought of as a *Space*. This chapter describes the different spaces and forces that death creates for individuals, families and communities, and offers a new conceptual model for reimagining compassionate end-of-life experiences.

Prior work

Numerous professions and practices have explored death and dying, and several initiatives and projects stand out as inspiring — both in their use of varied design formats and the diversity of approaches emerging from different cultures and geographies.

Professor Larissa Hjorth of RMIT in Australia conducts *digital ethnography on grief and loss*, recognising the fact that mobile media is deeply embedded in our everyday lives and is being used in personal and public rituals of mourning. In particular this is vividly clear in evolving practices around mortality, memory and memorialisation[1].

Meanwhile in the US, filmmakers John Bruce and Pawel Wojtasik trained as death doulas in preparation for their *documentary End of Life* that journeys with five terminally ill people at different stages of death. Its immersive approach invites us as viewers to explore our own body, senses and ability to be present with facing our own mortality[2].

Humor can also be used to reset our expectations around death; radical philanthropy organisation Lien Foundation's *Life Before Death campaign* in Singapore includes the stigma-shattering project *Happy Coffins* — pairing hospice residents with artists to co-design each resident's coffin inspired by their life story, hopes and wishes[3].

Finally, the *Death Tech Research Team* is a group of anthropologists, social scientists and human-computer interaction specialists in Australia whose projects include Disposal of the Dead and Future Cemetary that explore alternatives to burial and cremation, and the role of new technologies to enhance the public experience of cemeteries[4].

This benchmarking demonstrates the opportunity to work on the topic of death at multiple levels of society — from the individual to national policy — and a need to collaborate across disciplines and contexts in order to achieve richer meaning and greater impact. It confirms the value in creating a shared space, vocabulary and set of principles for such collaboration. What role and responsibility can design and design research bring? We see our reframing of Death as a Space as an initial contribution to the debate.

Death isolates

For terminal patients in the process of dying, death is *isolating*. When someone faces a terminal illness it is not unusual for people around them to feel at a loss for what to say or do. Most of us are not prepared or equipped for these kinds of conversations, no matter how close our relationship is to the person; they may seem wrapped in a space that we struggle to enter, partly because as a society we never intentionally visit this space, in fact we often consciously try to avoid it.

As a result, these implicit cultural and explicit communication barriers can render a person isolated in the moment to face death; without finding new ways to reach them in this space, we risk assuming that they do not have clear plans, choices, hopes and preferences for their future. Because even at the end of life there may still be a form of future to consider, albeit shorter. And we risk not being able to care for them as fully, and to express our love as deeply as we might want.

From the point-of-view of the caregiver, the loss of a loved one naturally triggers a highly personal, inner emotional response. One that is hidden from view, experienced first and foremost in our own private, intimate world. This potentially also leaves us isolated from others in our individual experience. How could someone else know and understand our pain, when we might even be struggling to do so ourselves?

For some, this hidden experience could feel safer and therefore easier to control. But even if we *wanted* to share our thoughts and feelings with those around us, we may not always feel we have the space, time or even the right words to express our thoughts around death in a way that feels authentic. How do we let others in?

Given the medicalisation of death, it is interesting to consider this effect in the healthcare sector where palliative care teams are usually multidisciplinary, with doctors working closely alongside specialist nurses, psychologists and medical social workers. Yet, in the moment to deal with specific tasks or procedures surrounding death, it is typically the doctor who is expected to take the lead — to deliver bad news to the family, to prescribe final palliative care, to sign the death certificate.

We have come to understand that not all doctors feel confident and comfortable to hold these difficult conversations with families at the end-of-life. In a recent project by The Care Lab with a network of private nursing homes in Spain we developed an end-of-life service protocol and training program/tools that enable the organisation as a whole to resist such isolation, by introducing new ways for staff to overcome their own fears and taboos around death and dying in order to better accompany their clients from admission all the way to the end of life.

Thus, professional practices can inadvertently create invisible communication barriers that prevent the wider care team from offering more holistic care to families facing end-of-life situations. And once medical processes render the person and their family passive in the experience, the space itself becomes over-professionalised, such that it can be hard to wrest back control and shape the circumstances around death, including planning funeral rituals in a more personal way.

How might we empower people to be able to bring others into the space of death with them?
Making time for conversations about death is a key strategy for inviting people into the space of death to reflect and discuss it together. Design research approaches and tools can help to create a moment in time for people to encounter the space of death; making an appointment to meet and to talk about their personal experiences

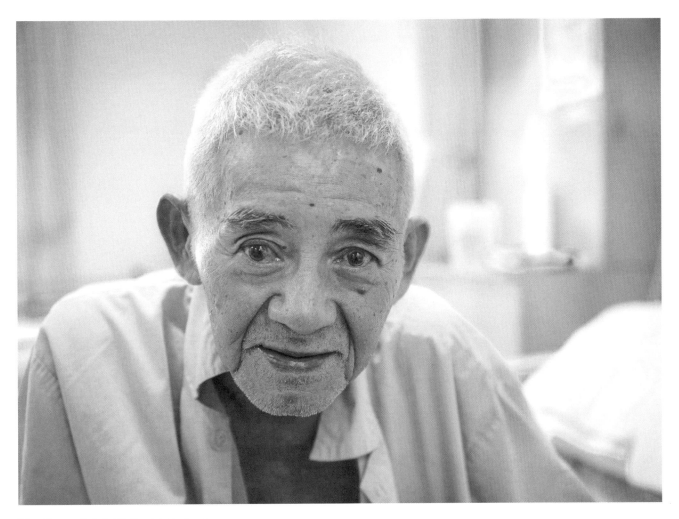

A dear Singapore Uncle that The Care Lab interviewed during the Hospitable Hospice project; he was one of thirteen terminally ill patients we met, and yet was the only one still alive by the end of the project. His image hangs in our studio as testament to why we work to transform Care.

safely, one to one with a researcher. In addition, and once inside the space, visual research tools can help to further lower the threshold for people to be able to begin their own storytelling and overcome personal fears and social stigmas in the process.

In design terms, this mechanism of opening up the experience of death from the individual to the community can be seen in The Care Lab´s program design strategy from the Hospitable Hospice project in Singapore; considering the moment when a family or friend experiences death as a natural touchpoint for individual reflection.

The design intention is to provide support and care to someone confronting death either as a caregiver, patient or professional. In order to do this we ourselves must be able to visit the space during our life, instead of letting it lie abandoned at the physical and conceptual 'outskirts' of most societies. If we can visit, explore, discover, reflect and inhabit this space of death we have the chance to also create an important opportunity for learning and growing together as a community — to honour this fundamental shared human experience. Replacing isolation with a sense of solidarity.

How might we facilitate compassionate conversations that help us to cope and heal some of our deepest wounds?
Design research methods can enable people to feel accompanied in their end-of-life journey. To momentarily feel less alone, and help build the kind of trust, empathy and compassion in relationships that could in turn enrich the current experience of life itself.

Are you afraid of being
a burden to your
family and others?

Top: A patient The Care Lab interviewed for the Hospitable Hospice project
decided to give their research incentive to his doctor; by chance we found her
carrying the gift the day after the interview, and realised patients need ways
to express gratitude to those around them. www.thecarelab.org/breaktaboos

Above: This end-of-life conversation toolkit by The Care Lab invites families to
an afternoon tea with a trained facilitator who gently guides them to consider
with each cookie a specific question around end-of-life choices.

HOW IT IS TODAY

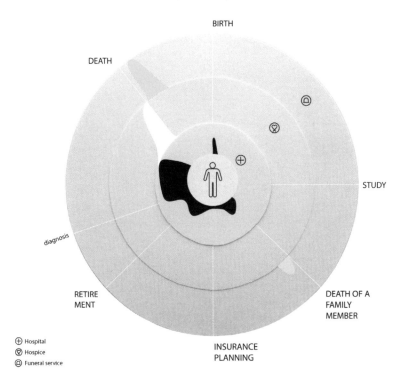

BIRTH

DEATH

STUDY

diagnosis

RETIRE
MENT

DEATH OF A
FAMILY
MEMBER

INSURANCE
PLANNING

⊕ Hospital
⊗ Hospice
⌂ Funeral service

HOW IT SHOULD BE

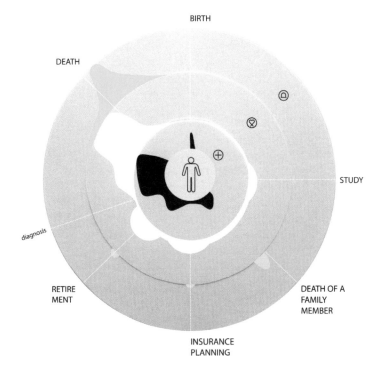

BIRTH

DEATH

STUDY

diagnosis

RETIRE
MENT

DEATH OF A
FAMILY
MEMBER

INSURANCE
PLANNING

End-of-life issues usually only surface when an individual is directly confronted with their own mortality,
which is usually too late for defining personal choices. This life stage-based model from The Care Lab´s
Hospitable Hospice work takes advantage of the moments when a community grieves, i.e. at funerals, to
raise the topic in families and provide a moment to reflect on individual end-of-life choices.

Death repels

As a topic to discuss and work with, death *repels*. It first isolates, but it perpetuates that isolation by actively preventing people from connecting with each other, from making decisions, and from interrogating their own opinions. The previous section showed that even those with the best intentions can feel unable to enter the space that death creates. It showed that people don't know how to discuss their circumstances or the situation, and that we've come to rely on medical language and terminology to even find a way into these difficult conversations.

If people don't know *how* to talk about death even when it's happening to them, then they certainly struggle to discuss death when they're healthy, fit, and have a reasonable expectation of not dying anytime soon.

Medicalising death reinforces it as an issue only to be discussed in clinical settings and with health professionals. It prevents families, loved ones and friends from broaching the topic and understanding the choices and decisions that are available to them. It is for these reasons that The Care Lab has been exploring the opportunity to break the taboos and intentionally design the end-of-life conversation experience; not only the topics and content, but also the interactions and rituals as well as the conditions in which a good end-of-life conversation can take place. This includes designing the actual moment to hold such conversations into the service blueprint itself.

In a project with the Australian Government, Paper Giant found that most people struggle to know how to raise the topic with their loved ones. This resulted in poor planning for death, which resulted in a more traumatic experience for those left behind after a death. Even if death was a topic of urgency, and needed to be discussed, we found in our research that people do not know how to interrogate their wishes or document their plans.

Talking about it with loved ones was one thing, but knowing what your options are with the end-of-life experience, and knowing what legal and medical decisions you needed to make ahead of time, were all difficult. This led to miscommunication between

loved ones, and even further traumatic experiences for families who disputed wills or the wishes of their departed loved ones. We found that death literacy was important — if you'd had a bad experience managing the loss of a loved one in the past, you were able to plan better next time.

The design challenge we identified was one of triggers, conversations and documentation.

———————————————

"We're all going to die, and it's something in Western civilisation we really don't talk about. We cling to the formalities and protocols of having a funeral and having a wake and all those sorts of things — it's like they're life buoys that keep you afloat. It's almost like when someone dies it's a terrible shock. We treat the whole thing about death like — if we don't talk about it or if we pretend it doesn't actually exist." Dean, participant in the 'Death of a Loved One' project

———————————————

How might we help people discuss the topic of death with their loved ones?

Rather than waiting for news of an imminent death, or needing to have a traumatic, poor experience of managing

"I decided to video my mum because I don't want to go through the legals and probate again, when the time comes."

Marina's father left his entire estate to her as documented in his will. He didn't tell his long-term girlfriend his wishes, and when he died, she contested the will. Resulting legal proceedings and probate processes compounded stress for Marina. As "insurance" against family squabbles in the future, Marina organised to video her mother in the presence of a lawyer. Marina, participant in the 'Death of a Loved One' project by Paper Giant

the estate of a loved one, it's important to design ways for sensitive, informed and meaningful conversations between individuals and their loved ones.

If we think of death as a space, designers have an opportunity to help people enter it but also explore it, sit with it, and embrace their agency within it. We found that it's hard for people to sit with the idea that they're going to die, and it's even harder to understand what it is that you want when it happens.

This was not only the case for individuals as private citizens — it was also true for individuals as professionals within government agencies and other service providers who have power over the experience of estate management. Whilst there is a valuable role for professional services to play in triggering conversations and decisions about the end of life (medical, yes, but also financial advisers and even funeral directors), we learned in our research that even professionals find it difficult to talk about death.

This has deep implications. Not only does it reinforce the topic as a medical consideration to only be discussed in clinical decisions, or by *certain professionals*, it also means that the wide gamut of services and training that are needed to manage the end-of-life, and to manage the estate of someone recently deceased, are often themselves under-designed.

As a result, services, responses

and procedures for dealing with the end-of-life are often much more poorly designed than more common, more profitable, 'customer journeys'. Whilst the onboarding experience for a service might be efficient and easy, 'offboarding' a customer who has died is often an obligation. The taboo-ness of the topic means that the service design around death is often overlooked for less emotional challenges.

If death is a space that *repels*, it prevents one more opportunity for redesign: How might we better support non-medical professions to have conversations about death?

"I think you do learn to deal with it on the job. Also I think part of it is inherent — it's either you know how to deal with it or you don't."
Andrew, lawyer

Death envelops

"Grief is different. Grief has no distance. Grief comes in waves, paroxysms, sudden apprehensions that weaken the knees and blind the eyes and obliterate the dailiness of life." Joan Didion, The Year of Magical Thinking

How might we help people grieve in their own way?
Death causes grief, and once a death has occurred, grief can consume and encompass a person's being. It envelops them. Grief, like death, can itself be thought of as a space that people inhabit and move through. People experience it differently and at different paces and intensities.

In 2018, Paper Giant conducted research with a trust of cemeteries in Melbourne, Australia's greater northern region. The focus of this research was to understand modern practices around grief and memorialisation, and to present opportunities for the cemeteries themselves, as organisations, spaces and infrastructures, to better support people through the process of grieving, and to adapt to new forms of memorialisation.

Our research showed that each person's grief — their internal response to loss — is unique; shaped by who they are and their individual circumstances. Still, across our dozens of interviews with people of different cultural and faith backgrounds, we came to understand three common needs that people have.

First, people have a need to grieve in personal ways. We found that everyone had different ways of acknowledging and processing loss, and that there was angst and anxiousness around how they should be perceived to grief. People needed help understanding that there was no right way to grieve.

Grief is enveloping, but it looks and feels different to different people. For designers, there is an opportunity to show people that grief doesn't have one true face.

"It was weird that none of us cried. I think some people may have found me too chirpy, but in my head I was just trying to cope"
Lucy, participant in the 'Death of a Loved One' project

"I'm the kind of guy who just moves on with things, but you still feel emotions. It's coming back [right now] as we're talking"
Michael, participant in the 'Death of a Loved One' project

"When death happens, you are out of your mind" Divya, participant in the 'Death of a Loved One' project

---

How might we help others respect and work with someone else's unique experience of grief?
The second universal need is related to support — and the need to have genuine expressions of support, no matter how grieve presents itself. We've already discussed how death repels — but even when support and conversations occur around a loss, it's important to people that they feel genuine and tailored. This is a need for both family and friends, but also professional services.

For designers, there is an opportunity to help others work with the unique grief that someone is inhabiting. If grief *envelops*, the challenge is not only to help others enter that space, but to acknowledge it's presence explicitly,

in the right ways for the context, and to respect the shape of it. Rather than thinking of grief as a problem to solve — as a stage to move someone through quickly, or to have a generic response to — it's important that mourners feel like they have genuine, personalised support.

"Soon after [my mother's] death, we spent a day with a family we are close to. But the whole day, they didn't mention Mum at all, which was very off. It has taught me that you should always say something to someone who is grieving" Lucy, participant in the 'Death of a Loved One' project

"The support was too artificial. It's like, when staff in Coles say 'have a nice day' but they don't know you! No one makes you feel comfortable when someone passes away. No one can do anything." Divya, participant in the 'Death of a Loved One' project

---

How might we create space for individuals to memorialise in their own ways, over time, with others? How might we enter this space ourselves carefully and sensitively?
The third and final universal need is honour and remember a loved one. Rather than thinking of grief as a short-term enveloping, it's important to acknowledge that it's often a space that people never — or do not want to — leave. Mourners need to create spaces of remembrance, where they can visit — physically, or emotionally. They need to be able to reminisce with others, to commemorate and feel connected to the loved one who has passed.

Like grieving, memorialisation is unique to individuals and their circumstances. For many, visiting a specific place, like a cemetery, gives them the emotional and mental space to connect with their memories of their loved one. People need to feel free to memorialise and remember in their own idiosyncratic ways. The opportunity for us, when thinking about death as a space that *envelops*, that people may never truly leave, is more hopeful and productive.

We have talked here about how death is an actor that sits between people and creates influenced *spaces*. Its influence is not the same for everyone, everywhere and these differences in expectations can create tensions and frictions around the experience itself — what death does, what it symbolises and how it can be navigated.

Discussing the death of her father, one of our research participants reporting on the memorialisation practices of her mother:

"Mum will light a candle at Dad's grave. She needs something tangible to make that connection with him. She has a candle lit for him at home as well, but being there, she says she always feels a sense of relief when she leaves [the cemetery]. It's like she's made contact" Cathy, participant in the 'Cemeteries Trust' project

Workshop participants discuss memorialisation and grief, as part of the GMCT project, Paper Giant.

Death, Dying and Covid-19

The pandemic created an opportunity for us all to reflect upon our state of wellbeing and emotional health, our relationships with those we care about, as well as at a more fundamental level what it means to be human.

As designers and researchers, we could also reflect upon the practices and experiences of working in the space of death, dying and end-of-life care. We saw, together with several of our clients and partners in this topic, the need to shift focus towards emerging new questions provoked by the pandemic — how were families coping to organise and celebrate funerals during lockdown? In what ways was the pandemic bringing the topic of death and dying into the home and how was this impacting children and families? What might be longer term effects on the mental resilience of exhausted frontline professionals?

As a result Covid-19 enriched our understanding of death as a space in the following ways:

Death isolates: We may have always lacked the vocabulary, confidence and skills to address these subjects and share our expectations and wishes. But now, we also lacked the physical space and comfort. Digital end-of-life experiences, including FaceTime farewells became a cruel reality during Covid-19.

Death repels: At a system level we saw care services behaving in strange ways around death; for example, under pressure of managing deaths during Covid-19, some UK hospitals had discharged patients to nursing homes, with deaths then occurring outside of their jurisdiction and resources. But there were failures to bring leadership, accountability, transparency and somehow also humanity to the experience in the most critical moment.

Death envelops: The pandemic, with it's lockdown or stay-at-home restrictions, made the space of grief and memorialisation more isolating. Often, loved ones couldn't be with each other at the moment of death. Attendance at funerals was often digitally mediated, and more than other times the process of grieving was disembodied. Even if we could share the experience with others, this sharing was distant, digital, and detached. The pandemic has elongated the processes of closure that bring peace after a death.

We continue to learn every day since the first lockdown because we have permanently entered the so-called *New Normal*, where the presence of death in our everyday life has become closer and more real. And with this so too does the opportunity to reframe the experience of facing death, to become one from which we can collectively grow and learn to appreciate more fully the life we are living in the present.

Our work has shown that death can be thought of as an actor that creates spaces between, around and through people. Rather than thinking about death as an event or as an attribute of individuals — as a problem to solve — thinking about death as a space, or as a series of different types of space, allows us to work productively with it, to identify different types of problems to work with and through.

When we as designers and researchers can enable others to inhabit the various spaces that death creates, to nurture a relationship with death while we are alive, we hope to demystify the topic and help others acknowledge it as a vital part of life: Will you step into the space of death with us and discover how it might strengthen you both professionally and personally?

1. Cumiskey, K.M. and Hjorth, L., 2017. Haunting hands: Mobile media practices and loss. Oxford University Press.
2. Visit https://www.digitaldeath.eu/
3. http://www.bothsidesnow.sg/
4. https://theconversationproject.org/
5. https://www.endoflifeproject.com/
6. https://deathtech.research.unimelb.edu.au/

#CareCapsules

Elin
Nurse & Family caregiver, NL

#CareCapsules

Miquel
Front-line doctor, Spain

1

1 Care Capsules

The Care Lab (Spain), STBY (Netherlands & UK), delaO design studio (Mexico), Quicksand (India), Matchboxology (South Africa), Somia CX (Indonesia & Singapore) and Summ()n (Russia & Netherlands)

The REACH Network started a multi-country initiative called Care Capsules that used video ethnography to capture people's lived experiences of care in the time of COVID19, touching also the topics of death and dying. Early 2020, the Covid-19 global pandemic quickly spread and affected the lives of billions around the globe, including the members of the Reach Network. We felt a strong need to come together as a community to collectively understand the changes in our societies at this unique moment in time. This resulted in the Care Capsules project, led by Reach partner The Care Lab in Barcelona and supported by Reach members from the UK, the Netherlands, Spain, Indonesia, India, South Africa, Mexico, and Russia. We

interviewed people with key roles (paid and voluntary) during the pandemic, and witnessed the emergence of a new understanding of care and new care roles in our global communities. Throughout this project, we looked at the pandemic with a more human- centred design approach, where the emphasis is placed upon how people actively find and grow resilience as a community in times of crisis from the bottom up. By collecting and analysing more than 50 personal stories and experiences of Covid-19 across the world, the Care Capsules project aims to learn about new ways of providing care to one another and how we can collectively redefine caring in our societies.

"I am more aware now about how busy life sometimes can be, combining time for family, work, and friends. Just take a pause, take more time for each other and really be there with your head and your heart."

2

2 Learning about death through design

Somia CX (Indonesia & Singapore)

"I witnessed my first death when I was in junior highschool. I remember my aunt came rushing to our home and asked me to play a video game with her in my bedroom. It was unusual, she had never asked that before. It was probably to distract me from seeing several strangers take my grandpa away in a stretcher. My grandpa suffered from a stroke and was finally relieved from his pain when he was 84 years old. Ever since I got quite obsessed with knowing where our consciousness goes after we die.

Recently, working at Somia CX gave me the opportunity to have a conversation about dying with 12 people in their 50s and 60s, and eight people from a younger generation. Initially, we were having a discussion to explore their perception towards retirement age, but it seemed that 'death' is an inseparable topic in this life stage.

3

4

3 Zero Suicide Lab

STBY (Netherlands & UK)

At the Zero Suicide lab organised for What
Design Can Do in Amsterdam, participants created
new perspectives on the issue of suicide among
middle-aged men. A relatively large amount of
suicide is currently committed among this risk
group, and 113, the Dutch national Suicide
Prevention is having problems reaching out to
these men. Lab participants investigated what
makes middle aged men vulnerable to committing
suicide, and at which moments in the lives of
these men they can be reached, even before they
develop suicidal behaviour.

4 Electrical bath duck

IDSL (France)

The 'Electrical bath duck' was a self-initiated
project by IDSL. Bringing the duck as a medium
to discussions generated useful feedback on
a difficult/heavy topic such as death and
suicide. The project also stimulated a lot
of online debate.

This section reconsiders entrepreneurship as a grassroots movement. Despite challenging conditions, *grassroots entrepreneurs* in all corners of the world are able to combine creativity, business strategy and social value creation in order to effect meaningful change. A groundswell that aims to balance one's need for commerce with one's respect for the environment and culture that surrounds them.

By drawing attention to the social life of a mission, the case studies in this section reveal that communities and businesses assemble their collective will, and many of the social uncertainties involved in a struggle to reclaim and revive latent value, resources, and people. Entrepreneurship as a central agent in what can be perceived to be a *just transition*.

The case studies also reveal hidden accounts of a fundamental urge to become better, and to make good things in difficult circumstances. The self-organized collective action of members of local communities steered by creative minds, shows us what regional resilience is, and how reviving and encouraging traditional and sustainable ways of living can be drivers of change.

Redefining communities through entrepreneurship

Kelvin Kaari & Cal Bruns (Matchboxology, South Africa) and Yuki Uchida (Re:public, Japan)

At a time when sustainability is a central topic in global discourse, innovative young entrepreneurs are leading the way in the thinking and designing of sustainable futures which in turn is redefining communities. Using creative and design thinking, they are drawing inspiration from existing resources to create social and economic value, driving much needed growth. The cases in this chapter highlight this curious trend, where young entrepreneurs are building products and services that are helping communities rediscover their social and economic potential.

These initiatives demonstrate the incredible capacity for entrepreneurship in re-thinking the concept of community in relation to robust economic output. Perhaps the key innovation among these cases is their resourceful use of existing knowledge and human capital to create value — which is unconventional in a world where we are constantly looking for new solutions. By looking back at traditional crafts in textiles, traditional cake making recipes, traditional artisanal bead work and rethinking how to drive market demand and generate social value, young entrepreneurs are giving a new lease of life to dwindling communities.

This is an emerging trend with the potential of challenging discourse and policy on pressing issues such as rapid urban — rural migration in developing countries, which is a real pressing problem especially in African states. It points us in the direction of retrospect as a collective, to really think of how we can leverage already existing crafts and neglected resources for community benefits at the civic and government level.

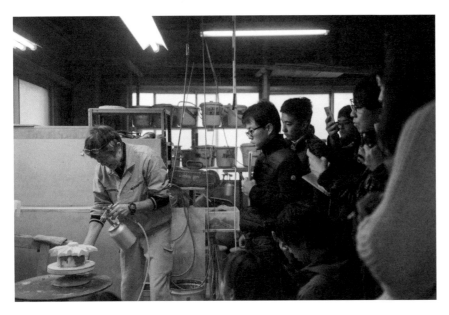

Xschool Fukui

Gone Rural Eswatini

XSCHOOL in Fukui: Reviving latent industries

Tokyo is Japan's most popular destination for young people looking to begin their careers. As is characteristic of big cities, Tokyo offers a fast paced eclectic lifestyle and numerous opportunities for professional development. However, the same allure is its undoing as unrelenting migration continues to congest the city thus compromising the quality of life — an unsustainable trend. Curiously, young people are moving to less popular destinations in Japan and applying their talents to revive latent industries, spurring economic and social prosperity in places with dormant economic potential.

Take for instance Fukui, a city of 260,000 people located on the Sea of Japan. Japan's mature economy and declining population limits resources for medium sized cities like Fukui. The local government of Fukui tasked Re:public to encourage consumer spending and tourism by publicising the city's strengths. Many regions' local governments within the country

have developed marketing campaigns to address similar concerns, but the team of Re:public/XSCHOOL took a different approach. In order to attract young creatives, they created a system that would yield projects and provide new value for local industries and communities through the rediscovery of latent value and the adaptive capacities of local resources and people.

Re:public aimed to make Fukui an attractive destination for young people looking for their next career opportunity. They built a 4 month long incubation program where local industry players from textile, fermented food industries and more, and diverse young creatives from in- and outside of the city came together to generate new ideas through the city's industrial background, history, and culture. XSCHOOL, supported by Fukui government, explores local industries, traditional craft resources, and multi-sector human resources as a platform for creating new projects. Several product and service businesses prototyped during XSCHOOL have been realized subsequently. In addition, the project has spawned a variety of other activities, such as the beginning of tourism in the textile industry and the establishment of incubation labs with XSCHOOL members in textile companies. This has attracted young creatives leading to the founding of new

projects and networks that are gradually making Fukui an exciting destination for young creatives and design thinkers.

While the products are important indicators, Re:public's broader goal in the design of XSCHOOL is to enhance the regional resilience of Fukui. The real impact lies in the revitalization of latent traditional crafts and industries that were once dormant and the ongoing transformation of the social fabric to one that is diverse, youthful and creative.

Going Rural & Northern Rangelands Trust: Sharing interests and values

In Africa, entrepreneurial concepts like Going Rural and Northern Rangelands Trust are breathing new life into rural communities struggling to maintain relevance and economic viability for future generations.

Going Rural has nurtured a vibrant young artisan community of 780 women across 52 Eswatini (previously known as Swaziland) villages by revisioning a traditional art that younger generations saw as 'that thing my grandmother does'. In 1992, Jenny Thorne saw an opportunity to refocus the traditional weaving craftsmanship she had observed in Eswatini with a contemporary design aesthetic that would appeal to Europeans. Over the years, Going Rural (which is in more aptly defined as a community) has enabled disenfranchised women to find sustainable self employment that supplies their household an income and allows them the flexibility to attend to traditional duties in their families. Going Rural's international retail clients are an integral and loyal part of this community, not as charity but as a mutually benefiting community of entrepreneurs with shared interests and values. Over the years, the Swazi artisans have taken complete leadership of the organization and regularly hold strategic meetings on the direction of the organization with their global clients. This virtuous community gives back to village communities across Eswatini by investing collective profits in initiatives such as clean water and HIV testing and treatment amongst all women members.

Northern Rangelands shares a similar model; it brought together over 1000 women across three tribes who are traditionally excellent craftspeople in traditional beadwork. As in Eswatini and Fukui, traditional skills were deeply embedded in the culture but younger generations were struggling to find interest and relevance in carrying on the traditions.. By bringing together a global community aesthetic with local artisan talent and modern marketing storytelling, Northern Rangelands has been able to rejuvenate the Samburu, Laikipia and Isiolo tribes in Kenya by designing and creating all beadwork that is sold to high paying clients and High Street retailers abroad. Bringing women from different communities has provided an opportunity for building bridges over some of the pertinent issues that in the past led to conflict. According to the Trust's founders, plans are underway to build a technical skills institution for the larger community, particularly targeting the youth.

What is evident in both Gone rural and Northern Rangelands Trust initiatives is the key role entrepreneurship has played in facilitating community building among women from divergent communities. Without such initiatives, it is possible that these new found communities of women would not exist and that old patterns of life would slowly die out.

Kuchen-stratsch: Rethinking community building for pensioners

Kuchenstratsch, German for "Cake chitchat", is a Munich based start-up founded by 22 year old Katharina Mayer. Having studied how to change society through business, Katharina started this initiative to help the fastest growing population in Munich (pensioners) make some extra money while providing a much needed social good service — baking of traditional cakes. Now retired folks make delicious traditional cakes which are sold in a cafe in Munich and can be delivered all over Germany.

Improving healthcare across the exploding retired population has placed tremendous stress on the government. Kuchenstratsch is an innovative opportunity to supplement the state pension while building a vibrant community amongst retired people, offering them a sense of independence, self worth and much needed community.

Kuchenstratsch is a physical and psychologically comforting community space; cakes made by "omas and opas" (german for grandmothers and grandfathers) connect young people with the older generation. In building community beyond the physical space into one built on smells, tastes and mutual value, one innovative entrepreneur has been able to contribute a sense of harmony to the changing population. Today, her social enterprise has a waiting list of omas and opas interested in becoming part of the bakery and the concept has garnered local and international media attention. Young people craving the comfort of oma's cake, and retired people looking for a sense of community are finding it at Kuchentratsch, where it has become increasingly common for people of all ages to congregate and share moments together.

Katharina Mayer von Kuchentratsch

1

2

1 Citizen-led transformations

Re:public (Japan)

Moment is a trans-local magazine that explores the future of cities created by RE:PUBLIC. The term "trans-local" refers to citizen-led transformations of environments and lifestyles that occur based on the reinterpretation of local technologies, resources, and cultures. Moment introduces such trans-local practices and practitioners from all parts of the world.

2 Documenting stories of resilience

Quicksand (India)

Quicksand's project with Bharat Mirle on documenting stories of resilience from in and around Bangalore, in light of the rapid expansion and environmental degradation in the city.

Buffalo Back Collective's work with marginalised communities living in the buffer zones of the Bannerghatta National Park at the edges of Bangalore. At the collective's workshop/farmhouse located in the area, women from the nearby villages in the buffer zone (including women from tribal communities) come together to produce, at a small scale, among other things, Ragi (finger millet) cookies, cooking vinegar, peanut butter and soaps. This product is then brought to market by the Buffalo Back Collective to be sold largely in urban areas such as Bangalore.

3 Designing caring communities

The Care Lab (Spain)

In a partnership between ELISAVA University Master's in Design and Communication, and the Barcelona Council Area of Social Rights, The Care Lab applied Service Design for Care as an approach to Social innovation, to explore how to

3

5

enable Caring Communities within the Barcelona Ageing Strategy enabled by the Social Superillas project. The following challenge was tackled: How might we create a platform to engage youth and eldery citizens to team up to Care for each other and their community?

As a one-day fieldwork research the students identified existing Care communities and potential Care exchanges spots in the superblock through a neighbourhood tour and observations. A co-creation session was organised with youth and elderly citizens, and family and professional caregivers; as well as 1-1 interviews to uncover their Care needs and capabilities, and identify opportunities for Care exchanges.

4 Community mapping

Apogee (Hong Kong)

Community map—As people get to know each other better, where people intersect and how they relate to characters, stories, experiences, and practices becomes clearer. These intersections show what practices connect and bind different roles and disciplines together. As the community's bonds become clearer, document them on a community map. Creating a community map gives you an idea of the strength of the relationships between certain people and show what those people value as a result. Discuss what these relationships mean for the people making the show and their practices.

5 Including micro-customers

Somia CX (Indonesia & Singapore)

One of the state-owned banks in Indonesia, wanted to increase the digital banking adoption for their micro customers. In this project, Somia CX's main challenge was to identify and create product concepts or interventions that encourage and help the micro customers (more specifically merchants) to adopt digital banking applications in fulfilling their needs through service prototyping and iteration in the field.

This section considers how designers may participate in global activism and how design researchers pave the way. It reveals how design practice works in some adventurous new settings, in which change is desperately needed. Rather than render an intimate view of local problems, it draws our imagination to powers associated with global scale. *Because this is an emergency, and life on earth is in crisis.**

In an attempt to counteract a destructive force such as climate change, joint efforts are needed. To catalyze change and shift harmful value systems, we have to act now and together on both global and local level. Excellent design research can show designers how to intervene with global problems within local realities without being naive, albeit with a good dose of positivity.

While studying the biggest challenges of our time: mass extinction and climate change, it is the responsibility of the design researcher to constantly alternate between the local and global and to point out how to navigate tensions, show problem areas, and highlight opportunities for design. This section shows the activist nature of collaborating Reach partners in order to motivate designers to design for the wellbeing of the planet firstly.

* Words used by Extinction Rebellion to indicate that we have a moral duty to take action and fight climate change.

Facing global climate challenges locally

Bas Raijmakers & Nina Stegeman (STBY, UK and Netherlands), José de la O (delaO design studio, Mexico), Ayush Chauhan (Quicksand, India) and Camila Boga & Kleber Puchaski (Flutter Innovation, Brazil)

The biggest global problems can greatly benefit from local efforts, and local challenges can benefit from a global view — this may range from climate change to how we deal with plastic waste. How can designers play a meaningful role in addressing global issues locally?

We have some experience with the 'Clean Energy Challenge' (launched in 2017-2018 by What Design Can Do (WDCD) in 5 cities around the world — Mexico City, São Paulo, Nairobi, Amsterdam and New Delhi), and the 'No Waste Challenge' (launched in 2021 in the same 5 cities plus Tokyo, and globally). Several partners from the Reach Network were involved in scoping and facilitating local challenges that all fed into the overall global WDCD challenges.

While describing these examples, we also explore the role of design research in facilitating local responses to global challenges through various stages of problem framing, multi-stakeholder collaborations, and co-creation workshops. Learning from each Reach partner's experience with the Clean Energy Challenge and the No Waste Challenge, and building on their own unique design research framework for addressing wicked problems of our times, the reflections in this chapter are applicable to a wider context of climate challenges.

Global+Local: Local submissions contribute to global impact

We strongly believe that creatives around the world can address global issues of climate emergency with meaningful local interventions and contributions. In order to create a global impact, we need lots of interventions around the world to drive change in the right direction. We are facing a global climate emergency: carbon dioxide levels and other greenhouse gases in the atmosphere are still rising and climate change is affecting every country on every continent. Climate change is a response of the planet to consumption and production patterns of large parts of humanity, including poor waste management. We have pushed our planet beyond its limits. All kinds of waste are threatening our ecosystems and biodiversity, with knock-on effects to climate change. We can not solve this global climate problem in one go. We have to solve this problem together. Different people and societies hold different pieces of the puzzle and it all needs to fit together. Together with What Design Can Do, we believe in the strong contributions design and creativity can make to transform societies.

In times of crisis, global institutions often have a reflex towards a top down almost militaristic approach to problems, which is quite deterministic. They tend to 'ignore' or underestimate the local resilience of communities and what they are capable of doing themselves. People are not passive 'victims' who are just waiting and sitting still until somebody comes to save them. Conversely, we often see in our work that amidst crises of different kinds, people are able to actually do something in many creative ways. Our role as designers and design researchers is to support that dynamic. At the same time, systemic problems do require a degree of institutionalised and centralised response as well of course, especially in the context of climate change. The Paris agreement is such an institutional response. The gap seems to be the inability of systemic responses to learn from and align with local ingenuity. Good science or good policy should be as human centered as good design is. And WDCD in its conception

as a global challenge anchored by strong local partners and expertise is a demonstration of how top-down and bottom-up approaches can indeed be in harmony.

The City Approach

The Clean Energy Challenge, launched by What Design Can Do (WDCD) in 2018, called upon start-ups, designers and students from all over the world to rethink how we produce, distribute and use energy in México City, São Paulo, Nairobi, Delhi and Amsterdam. The Clean Energy Challenge was the second WDCD Climate Action Challenge the global Reach Network supported. STBY (UK/The Netherlands) as global and local research partner, and Quicksand (India), delaO design studio (Mexico), and Flutter (Brazil) as local research partners. Before announcing the winners, STBY went through many different stages together with WDCD, and the main funder IKEA Foundation.

The first step in compiling a design challenge is doing foundational research. STBY initially explored the topic focusing on global climate science to set the scope and agenda for the challenge, and then worked with local research partners from the Reach Network to define the final briefs that were most relevant to each city. These briefs were the starting point for the participants in the challenge.

Early on in the research process for the Clean Energy Challenge we decided to focus on a city approach, as this would increase the impact of the challenge and enlarge the chance that submissions can actually be implemented. Studying existing reports, it became clear that cities consume over two thirds of the world's energy and contribute to more than 70% of global CO_2 emissions. In addition, cities are becoming more prominent in the fight against climate change, and mayors have a strong voice in decision and policy making. Around the world, C40 cities are taking bold climate action, leading the way towards a healthier and more sustainable future. Throughout the research we also noticed that mayors

were more responsive to climate change than national authorities.

A final reason for focussing the challenge on cities, is that WDCD wanted to support the winners of the Clean Energy Challenge with an acceleration program. Therefore we needed to have a local network. Building local networks is crucial for the change we want to achieve with the Climate Action Challenges. We started with building these local coalitions already from the beginning of the research by interviewing local domain experts and by extending these coalitions through organizing local workshops to gather local input for the briefings.

In order to trigger and catalyse change, the global design challenges aiming for local entries need to be based on excellent global and local design research. Only then the winning projects can be successfully implemented into local realities. Often, design contests use briefs that are very general or offer a Western perspective, and do not always fit within local realities. It is often unclear, or not addressed how to implement those general or 'global' solutions into different localities. With the research in preparation of WDCD challenges, we start with the latest global climate science, followed by local research to understand the context of particular cities and their local challenges. The challenges should build on the latest science as much as on actual needs of people and the planet in different local environments.

A key principle in doing foundational research on global complex issues is constantly alternating between these local and global perspectives. This global+local approach is needed, because the global and local are intrinsically connected. Therefore it is important to take into account any relevant local resources, possibilities and barriers while researching a global problem. Only then designers can create a bespoke response to a global emergency that could be scaled up while respecting local differences. A one size fits all blanket solution will have less impact.

The No Waste Challenge

The No Waste Challenge, launched by What Design Can Do in 2021, was the third climate action challenge in partnership with the IKEA Foundation. This global design competition focused on the impact of waste and consumerism on climate change. It was launched in the midst of another crisis: the COVID-19 pandemic. The two are however connected. Human destruction of ecosystems and biodiversity loss are creating virus spillover events, like COVID-19, much more likely. Our current wasteful lifestyles aren't just making the planet sick, they are making us sick too.

Designers and creative entrepreneurs around the world were invited to submit innovative solutions to reduce waste and to re-design our systems of extraction, production, and consumption to be less destructive — or even to make them restorative. Designers in particular are great at making future values more tangible, as visual stories that inspire people, organisations and societies to take a different course. To fight climate change and pollution behaviours and industries, we need interventions at various scales. Micro and meso sustainability focuses on the smaller actions that collectively result in a large environmental impact. Micro-sustainability is about individual efforts, behavior modification and changing attitudes, which create a more environmentally conscious individual or community. Meso- sustainability is about changing policies, processes, information systems and ways of doing things. These community-level actions have immediate local benefits. If they are widely imitated, they have a cumulative broader impact at the macro scale of organizational and even national policies and institutional change. Bottom-up small-scale approaches will not be enough on their own. We also need design to help shift the value systems in which current micro, meso and macro systems are embedded.

We as Reach Network believe that through doing this kind of work, we can show people around the world that design can help create a better world. WDCD design challenges show what design can do beyond creating beautiful objects or products with a short life span. Designing for a better world is quite unknown in many parts of the globe. There are still lots of people who think that design is about beautification, or embellishment, and not much more than that. The way that design is perceived in Mexico for example, is still very much focussed on beautification of objects, luxury, and bringing an aesthetic value into things. This is mainly because design is very much associated with interior design, and the design of products. Concepts as 'design strategy', 'design thinking', and 'design as a methodology' are not widely known. In another context like India, design has historically had roots in the rich tradition of crafts, but the industrial or post industrial society has failed to learn from these indigenous systems or practices. There is a whole vocabulary of design methods and mindsets — such as 'frugality', 'self sufficiency', 'decentralised', 'sustainable', that can be added to the global lexicon of design strategy.

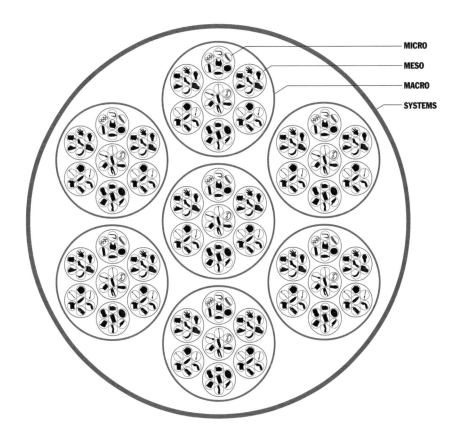

Seeking small hacks and big dreams. We need interventions at various scales.

Foundational Research: Exploring and scoping as a first step towards design briefs

Most designers start a design process with scoping. However, climate change is such a big topic that you cannot expect every designer who wants to do something about it, to start their own scoping. That is why we create and provide design briefs as input for the Climate Action Challenges. At STBY, we crunch the enormous pile of data that is available and identify initial problem areas and opportunities for design within this data. We start the research with a global perspective, while not ignoring local initiatives and perspectives. This foundational research usually entails a lot of exploratory and open desk research: reading UN-reports, collecting infographics, sketching and visualizing data, and having conversations about what we read with multiple stakeholders, experts and designers. Through this process we are gradually able to identify problem areas and opportunities for design.

Step 1 — Unpacking official reports to find out where effort is needed
The first step in doing foundational research into climate emergencies is to unpack extensive and dense UN-reports[1] and other scientific reports, and to make that kind of knowledge accessible and relevant to designers by converting the scientific, policy based data into accessible stories, insights and frameworks that all people (not just designers) can engage with. We first look at who are scientific authorities in the field so we can stand on their shoulders. The benefit of starting with studying UN-reports is you'll find out how scientists are looking at this problem globally, where they think effort is needed, and what the big categories of the climate problem are. In addition, these UN-reports offer knowledge about global, but also about regional and local emergencies. They offer lots of world maps with all kinds of details about regional and local emergencies. There is clearly a global economy nowadays, but there is also a global ecology, and already for much, much longer. Through studying the world

maps in these global reports you realise that if you do something in one place, it has an effect in another place. That is why it is important to look at how global, regional and local issues and developments connect, and to study the relationships between them. You can not study the global while ignoring the local. When you do research on a global level, you should focus on the relationships between different levels. For example; the climate problem is caused in different places (e.g. The Netherlands) than where it is felt most (e.g. Kenya).

Only focussing on the local level would be a mistake, because then you are not taking into account how it's all connected. Climate change and global warming are issues that are too big for a strictly local approach. The global and the local that we study can be seen as yin and yang. They are actually complementary, interconnected, and interdependent, and may give rise to each other as they interrelate to one another. That is why we scope the research with a global perspective, while not ignoring local initiatives and perspectives.

Step 2 — Sketching and visualising help to understand complex information better
It is often quite daunting to get your head around all the data, because academic and policy literature such as UN-reports have hundreds and hundreds of pages. Even summaries are pretty long. The UN uses a lot of infographics to explain what is happening and what will most likely happen in the future. Design researchers make use of design tools and methods to comprehend the data, such as sketching and visualising data. We may sketch diagrams to show relations between what's happening in the sea and what's happening on land for example. Visualisation is a strong tool to analyse a situation. Infographics, for instance, are very helpful both as input and output for design research. Visualization helps to summarize and understand complex information better.

Sometimes the first iterations of those visualizations that we make during the scoping of the challenge, end up in the What Design Can Do design briefings in the end. A good example is the 'Energy Bagel' diagram (see page 31) that we sketched for the Clean Energy Challenge[2]. It shows the connection between sustainable energy, energy poverty and 'energy decadence' in one image. Visualisation of what we learn from very early on is important to get an understanding of complex issues. We often use tools from generally available resources such as the DIY toolkit[3] as well. For example the Causes Diagram that helps to distinguish the symptoms and causes of the problems that we address. We also look for existing models that can help us to understand the problem better, such as the circular economy[4] for instance.

Step 3 — Having continuing conversations along the way to deepen understanding
Doing design research is not just about reading, writing and sketching. Another element that is important while researching complex global issues is engaging in regular conversations about the topic you are researching. While doing the explorations and clustering, we initiate lots of conversations: among ourselves (the research teams), with What Design Can Do, the IKEA Foundation, and different teams within the Reach Network, as well as discussions with specific domain experts. We always make an effort to reach out to a mix of experts (subject matter experts, design experts, policy experts) in order to figure out where impact is most needed, where there is already local momentum, and where design can make the most relevant and strongest impact. Through these conversations you deepen your understanding of a topic, because you can test some insights that you have.

For instance, for the No Waste Challenge we asked feedback on the global draft brief from 25 experts and designers around the globe. We shared the draft briefing with them and asked to answer some questions. With 5 of them, STBY did an in-depth follow up interview to really learn what could be improved. STBY analysed the feedback and learned that overall people thought the brief in general was open, inspiring, exciting and very clear. The (take-make-waste) structure that we chose seemed to work well. This structure offers both possibilities for different designers and to determine the potential of an initiative. However, in lots of low income countries and emerging economies there is a huge informal waste economy that deals with reuse of products, for instance. We received very valuable feedback about the structure that would benefit from a more clear 'informal economy' perspective (of bartering, gleaning, repair and DIY) that is equally important as the 'formal economy' (founded on a take-make-waste model and starting to transition to a circular economy).

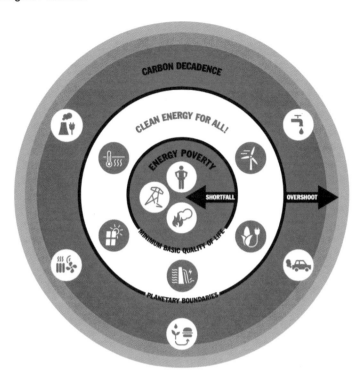

The Energy Bagel diagram shows the connection between sustainable energy, energy poverty, and energy decadence.

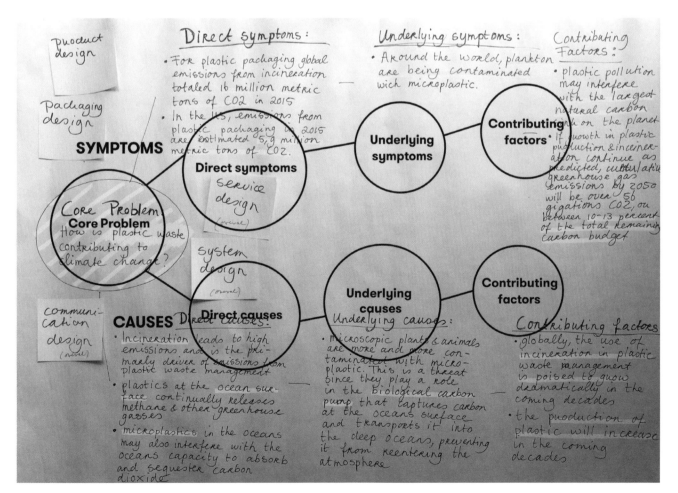

The Causes Diagram helps you think of a problem in a thorough manner and provides a structured way to analyse it

Local Workshops: Creating local feedback and perspectives

In the run up to global challenges we often organise and facilitate local co-creation workshops in places where the local research is taking place. These workshops are a crucial tool in the research process, as they localise the global model and the foundational research. The general scope of the challenge and the specific design briefs greatly benefit from these workshops, as they generate local feedback and perspectives on the foundational research in which we primarily gain a global perspective on the topic and issues (while not ignoring the local). This global perspective offers a high-altitude bird's eye view on things, while the local perspectives from the workshops in many different places make the research become truly international. This results in relevant and meaningful local briefs, and often also in new local collaborations with experts and creatives.

Finding out what resonates locally
For the Clean Energy Challenge, Reach Network partners delaO design studio, Flutter, Quicksand and STBY organised workshops in Mexico City, São Paulo, Nairobi, Amsterdam and New Delhi, inviting local experts and creatives to collectively examine the Energy Bagel, the main diagram that came out of the foundational research, and change it if needed. Local workshops explored the different energy domains that we found during the foundational research as a preparation for the Clean Energy Challenge. These domains were mobility, heating and cooling, food, and building for example. We wanted to find out what resonated with designers and experts locally. The briefs that eventually came from this were very much domain related. The workshops were at the forefront of the final contextualised design briefs. We turned the outcomes of the workshops into five different draft briefs that were all focussing on different energy domains.

Online workshops due to Covid-19
The local research for the No Waste Challenge coincided with the Covid-19 crisis, in the second half of 2020. Local desk research and interviews were done locally by local teams from the Reach Network (except Tokyo), but mostly online. We were also not able to organise local workshops where people could meet in person. Online workshops for the local research about waste and consumerism in Mexico City, São Paulo, Nairobi, Amsterdam, New Delhi and Tokyo were organised. STBY provided a workshop pack which could be used during the workshop and was locally translated. The online workshops were preceded by desk research and expert interviews on local relevant themes, problem areas and opportunities and design examples dealing with waste and consumerism. The local research was used to create local city perspectives which were local representations and supplements to the global briefs on Take, Make and Waste.

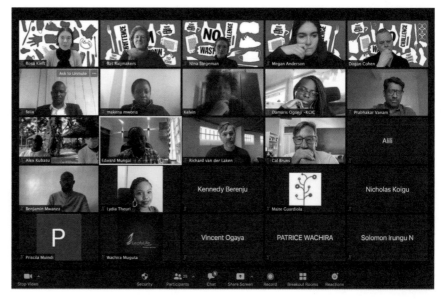

Local workshops in Amsterdam, Mexico-City, New Delhi, Nairobi and São Paulo, and a design jam in London and Amsterdam

Navigating Tensions: Engage rather than avoid

As mentioned above, addressing climate change in and through cities is more urgent than ever. However, the urban context of climate change can be messy, because of the many vested political and economical interests. This is where local research comes in. It is the design researchers role to uncover and mark out these messy situations. It doesn't really help much to only find the well organised, clean, and perfect situations, because there is not that much to change there. The local research for the challenges is therefore focussed on uncovering problem areas and tensions, in order to spot opportunities for design. The world is not divided into good and bad. There is a grey space in between that we need to deal with, sometimes called 'the movable middle'. This is where most change can actually happen. In addition to climate change, social justice is another topic WDCD wants to address in its challenges. That is why we bring social justice into the research conversations too. We address social topics such as waste pickers, and energy poverty too while studying waste, consumerism and clean energy. We should engage in conversations about difficult and messy topics as opposed to avoiding them. We have to show tensions and complexity, because often these topics are not easy to deal with. Design needs to be bold in engaging in conversations that are outside its comfort zone. And therefore it is important to surround itself with people and experts that the discipline of design may not typically engage with. These are topics such as human rights, politics, and grassroot movements. These unexpected quarters are where uncomfortable questions will be raised and designers need to build the capacity to engage with these questions and find a way of addressing them (if not resolving them) in its practice.

Tensions are useful in research

Tensions help us to sense and unpack what is happening; what is going on in different contexts, and to inform ourselves about what to deal with on a local level. As researchers it is not our role to tell WDCD and the designers attracted to the Climate Action Challenges what they should do, but it is our role to tell them what to deal with. We show them what is happening and tell them there are certain things they need to know and to deal with. The challenges need to be funded by multiple partners, so especially when WDCD is looking for local (and global) funding, they have to push a lot of agenda's. WDCD needs to know about the dark side of the recycling industry in some localities for example. Such tensions help the organisational part and the development of the challenge. Tensions help WDCD in making decisions about who to partner with for example, and how to model the campaign around the challenge. Tensions are something to engage with rather than avoid, and they are quite important to acknowledge for design as a discipline for changing the world too. Often, where tensions exist, change is also possible because the situation is not stable. In conversation with all researchers involved in the local research in the different cities, we identified three types of tensions to deal with while doing local research about global climate challenges: the tensions between the global and local, tensions that have to do with inequality, and the tension between different parties involved in the challenge with different interests.

Tensions between different dominant narratives

The global design challenges usually touch on various interconnected global and local problems. At the same time, each society and culture where these problems play out has different dominant narratives. While the local engagements bring you the depth on particular issues, the global perspective prevents you from being swept away by what might be a dominant narrative in a specific context. Often, there are certain narratives that dominate when you look at a particular culture and a particular context. For example in India, the current dominant narrative is around the informal economy, and how that has a role to play. Often you cannot solve problems in a local context, unless you are able to get into the weeds, into what the most pressing issues are. At the same time you realise that the global perspective actually rounds off the problem really well, with all the other dimensions that it brings, because cultures are different. Tensions between what one culture and one economy or one context needs, as opposed to what might be perceived as a global good is what we are looking for in the local research stage. Local nuances are sometimes aligning with the global perspective, but often they are also contrasting.

Feeling squeezed between the rather western perspective and local realities

The STBY team was responsible for both the global research and the local Amsterdam research, and also for the coordination of the local research in the other cities. We sometimes felt squeezed between the global and the Amsterdam perspective, and the different local perspectives that the other local researchers came up with. The most clear example of that is when the circular economy came up as a potential solution to the waste problem during the global research for the No Waste Challenge. We realised that this was probably a rather Western perspective on the waste issue, and that it was not sufficiently taking into account informal economies for example. The circular economy seemed a top down big system idea that would work in a country like the Netherlands, and the city of Amsterdam. The city of Amsterdam had indeed adopted a strategy called 'Amsterdam Circular'. However, we were hesitant to bring this idea of a circular economy into the global brief. With the results from the local research in other cities, this idea was confirmed. For example, in India Quicksand found that sustainability and circular economy are largely 'borrowed concepts'. Our perceptions of efforts that could make things sustainable, may disregard other efforts that are already established in other local contexts.

From a 'take-make-waste' economy towards a just and circular economy

The desk research on waste

and consumerism led us to the understanding that global heating is caused by the collection of raw materials, the transformation of these materials into products that are used briefly and then discarded as waste. It is important to realize that next to the production of waste and greenhouse gasses, each phase of the take-make-waste model uses resources like water and energy as well as land that is no longer available for biodiversity and CO_2 absorption. This insight resulted in an infographic of the current economic 'take-make-waste' model which is used to structure the global briefing of the No Waste Challenge. To bend the take-make-waste line, we must focus on where it matters most, we need a just and circular economy.

Tension between different interests and agendas
In The Netherlands, the government is providing tools to rank and prioritize strategies towards a circular economy. The R-ladder is such an instrument, the higher on the ladder, the more impact the strategy has, is the idea. In the Dutch context this works, since it is part of national policy documents, but not in all countries the government does provide useful instruments and policies to deal with waste. Innovation is not pursued everywhere in the world, hidden agendas and practices may lead instead. Sometimes there may even be a link between sustainability and corruption. In Mexico the research of delaO design studio showed that the pathways that creative people should take, have to overtake institutions, like public institutions and government, and to come up with a solution that is viable. Instead of the government supporting citizens with providing resources for sustainable innovation, a lot of information about the dark side of the recycling industry came up during the research. The R-ladder does not fit within the Mexican context, and nor does it fit within the Brazilian context as local researchers of Flutter showed.

Tensions between different socio-economic levels
During the local research of the No Waste Challenge, we encountered a great deal of frugal design solutions from people with no resources. We noticed that many great solutions already exist, but they do not get the same attention as much more wasteful products or services the design industry is pushing. There is inequality between the 'creative elite' and people living in poorer conditions that come up with very creative solutions to deal with in their everyday struggles. This should be incorporated in the challenge briefing as well. The local perspectives should show the great solutions that are already out there and point out where design can still make a change, or help strengthen and learn from existing great solutions. Similarly, the Indian research conducted by Quicksand and the Japanese research outcomes made clear that several traditional approaches that are almost forgotten deserve renewed attention too. Researchers should be aware of who is really at the receiving end, who is the most vulnerable, and who has the ability to make a change. If we look at waste and inequality for example, then we see that it is being interconnected so deeply, not just at a local level, but at a much larger scale. An example of inequality regarding waste in the Dutch context for instance is that people at the lower economic end are wasting a lot more than people with more economic resources. You can hardly blame them, because living a sustainable lifestyle is quite expensive in the Netherlands. And then still, you might question what is even a sustainable lifestyle lived by the middle classes if they fly on long haul holidays at least once a year? We endeavoured to include this inequality between what people can do at different economic ends, into the discussion and challenge brief as well.

Delivering final contextualised design briefs
Using the outcomes of local research and workshops together with the foundational global research, STBY created the final briefs for the Climate Action Challenges. At this point again, we try to balance global and local. For the two different challenges discussed here we decided on slightly different balances, together with WDCD. The Clean Energy Challenge was focused on five cities with a separate brief for each city, addressing energy and food (Nairobi) or energy and mobility (São Paulo), et cetera, and less so globally because WDCD decided to focus on setting up local acceleration programmes for the winners in five cities. For the No Waste Challenge WDCD wanted to combine city acceleration programmes with a global track, which became feasible through a partnership with the global network of Impact Hub. This required a global brief, or actually three focused on Take, Make and Waste, the main framework that came out of the research. Next to that, six city perspectives on the global briefs were offered as separate briefs that complemented the global briefs. For designers submitting for other locales, the city perspectives offered insight into how the global brief could be localised. All briefs have a similar structure. They begin with a general introduction that gives the broad picture and defines several terms. Gradually, the briefs dive deeper into the issue at hand in each city, formulating one or more key questions and suggesting several important opportunities as starting points for designing. In selecting these we also look at what different design disciplines can contribute, from awareness campaigns to sustainable products and services, and transforming systems. Finally the briefs provide a good amount of background information including links, also to projects already in place. The intention is that with these briefings we provide the designers with enough open space to invent new approaches, but at the same time with the focus and support that helps them to be really effective and come up with meaningful solutions.

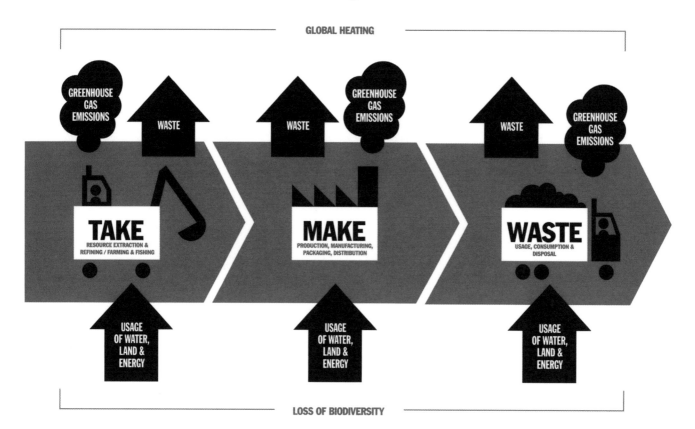

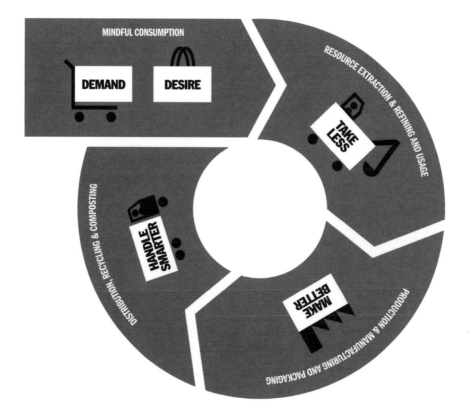

Top: The current economic 'take-make-waste' model
Bottom: A circular economy is restorative and regenerative by design.
It prevents waste by reusing raw materials in closed circles.

Launch: Sparking international submissions and supporting successful implementation

After the launch of a Climate Action Challenge by What Design Can Do, there are a couple of months until the deadline for submissions. WDCD creates a global campaign, building on the research to create the briefs. This requires translating nuanced and detailed research into slogans, which is another tension to navigate. Here it pays off to have clear different roles and responsibilities. Campaigning is another skill than researching. However, a big role of research and subsequent outputs is to make these accessible for people, and in some sense making it easier for marketing and communication teams to amplify it. The take-make-waste model was simple enough to communicate the No Waste Challenge, and this was abundantly discussed during the research stages. WDCD developed on top of that one of the key slogans "I am a bad designer" delivered by famous designers from the participating cities. This brought a strong design focus to the challenge that

was ironic and attracted attention, yet played on the responsibility a designer has as the research made abundantly clear. The strong partnership between WDCD, STBY and the Reach Network has created a mutual trust that allows us to challenge each other and collaborate on how to tell the stories about the challenge to different audiences in different contexts.

Beside telling stories, doing is also very important during the campaign. All Reach partners involved in the collaboration with WDCD are initiating and championing as many design jams as possible at different places to invite local submissions. These design jams, taking place at meetups, conferences and schools, are important for a few reasons: to promote the challenge so designers know about it, to bring creatives together so they can collaborate as a team, and to give them the opportunity to play with the idea of submitting. By delivering the informative and inspiring briefing pack to designers,

organising local collaborative design jams, and running the WDCD Climate Action Challenges, we play an important role in educating designers on sustainable, and systemic change. By inspiring them, and showing them how they can create things that can both help people and the planet, we are helping to change the design discourse, and thereby change the meaning and role of design.

The winning teams receive a project budget as well as tailor-made guidance to further develop their project during the acceleration phase of the challenge. The accelerator is aimed at giving the winners the tools to take their project to the next level. In each of the focus cities, a local partner organises sessions to help the teams connect with relevant partners, finances, customers and networks that can help bring their solution to market. This part of the Climate Action Challenges evolves with each iteration as well. For the Clean Energy Challenge, ten of the winners were also invited to Amsterdam for a one-week Bootcamp. Here they learned how to strengthen each team's entrepreneurial skills and what it takes to build businesses that focus on sustainable outcomes. For the No Waste Challenge, a new partnership with Impact Hub is expected to provide local acceleration support in many more locations. After the acceleration phase the winning projects are expected to be ready to 'make it happen', and have an operation running (often a social enterprise) that is close to the final implementation and go-to market of their ideas, so their work contributes towards a more sustainable and just world with less carbon emissions.

CARBON TILE
INDIA

Carbon Tile is the world's first tile made from upcycled carbon, fusing low-tech crafts with modern technology.

READ MORE

DAPODA: DESIGN LIVING LAB
BRAZIL

A group of designers and architects from the University of São Paulo decided not to let perfectly good wood go to waste and created Dapoda — a 'living lab' for circular design.

READ MORE

HAGAMOS COMPOSTA
MÉXICO

Hagamos Composta offers an alternative for families and businesses who want to handle their waste responsibly but do not have the knowledge, tools, or space to do so.

READ MORE

LEAFYLIFE
KENYA

LeafyLife is a new technology using an energy-efficient chemical process to turn dirty diapers into clean fuel.

READ MORE

LIVING COFFIN
THE NETHERLANDS

Loop is the world's first fully biodegradable casket made out of mycelium fungi.

READ MORE

MAPU SPEAKERS
GERMANY

Mapu Speakers is a line of eco-friendly sound systems made using natural materials like clay, wood, cork and wool.

READ MORE

Some of the winners of the What Design Can Do No Waste Challenge. See all winners at whatdesigncando.com.

1 Reports from the Intergovernmental Panel on Climate Change (IPCC) and The Intergovernmental Science-Policy Platform on Biodiversity and Ecosystem Services (IPBES).

2 Knight, S, Raijmakers, B, Draw and discover, sketching and mapping as a versatile tool across research stages, Explorers, thoughts on mapping in design research (2020)

3 https://diytoolkit.org

4 Ellen MacArthur Foundation (https://www.ellenmacarthurfoundation.org/publications)

1

1 'Plastic: Villain or hero?'

delaO design studio (Mexico)

As part of Primer 2020 and our platform Desde Casa, delaO design studio organized a speculative design challenge, Plastic: villain or hero?, that invited young designers to reflect on the use and value of plastics in relation to the pandemic needs. Participants design diegetic prototypes for two different scenarios.

Scenario 1: Bye bye plastics. Welcome to the new era, is a scenario in which plastic has been banned since 1992. In this scenario, researchers and environmentalists showed the low results of environmental regulations at a congress on sustainable development. In this scenario they showed the increasing production of plastics and their effects on the environment. Since then, plastic became the material of the past and marked the beginning of a new century that was driven by a feeling of sustainability in many countries.

Scenario 2: Plastic, the material that saved millions of lives, is a post-covid scenario in which the pandemic is over and people celebrate New year's eve with reflecting on pandemic experiences and learnings. They are remembering those who died because of COVID and thank the heroes who helped so many people to stay alive. Not only health workers and many other professionals were revered since the pandemic. Also, materials, objects, and clothing that were considered as a symbol of survival, including plastic. Therefore plastic recovered its force as an active, economical, and safe material after the pandemic.

2

2 Making households more sustainable

STBY (Netherlands & UK)

As part of the 'Plastic Unfantastic' project STBY conducted an auto-ethnography study of 12 days, following 24 participants through various moments of their lives. We used the Experience Fellow app, installed on the participants' mobile phones, to digitally 'follow' them during the research period. They were invited to report their encounters with plastic, describe their thoughts and feelings, take pictures to illustrate their experiences, and to score their satisfaction. Many reported plastic packaging as a major problem they face, and some illustrated how they create their own solutions to avoid using plastic.

Another project on sustainability was a large-scale national program to transition the use of energy in the Netherlands from natural gas to electricity, the Dutch government is eager to learn from early adopters and to identify ways to better support the many people and households who are still to follow. To inform this process of learning and support the development of new policies and services, STBY was invited to conduct a design research project across the country. One of the main insights regarding the transition process is that it is hardly ever a linear process. From the perspective of the residents, they are in most cases gradually on their way to make their homes more sustainable, and switching from natural gas to electricity is just one step in that process.

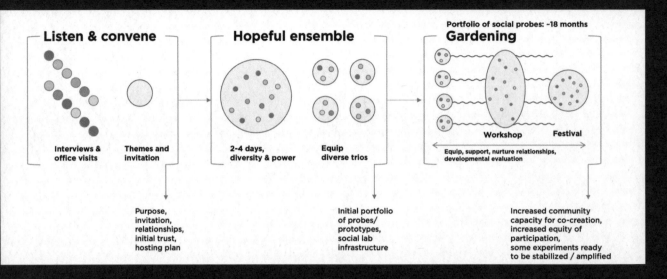

3

3 Holding social space for long-term change

Fit Associates (US)

When efforts involve many stakeholders, affect whole communities and systems, and intend outcomes that are more social than technical, they require a "container" that looks much different than typical project management. When there are multiple centers of power and fragmented points of view, it is essential to pay explicit attention to cultivating relationships and trust. When the challenge is too complex for any single solution, we need to support the emergence of desirable surprises from within the community. And when we seek to include people who have historically been omitted from participation, we need time to grow the community's capacity to gather and create afresh. We find it wonderfully helpful to sketch "participation strategies"– visual

representations of long-term, large-scale co-creation—as tools for imagining together and coordinating multistakeholder efforts over time. The picture represents two years of effort to transform the cultural patterns on a university campus. While the details naturally change as the life of the work progresses, the diagram represents agreement on intended outcomes and the overall shape of an approach to emergent strategies that center equity, inclusion, and community empowerment. And it shows the flow of concern for those who "hold the space" of relationship, conversation, and personal and group development that is so necessary for such work and so frequently omitted from plans.

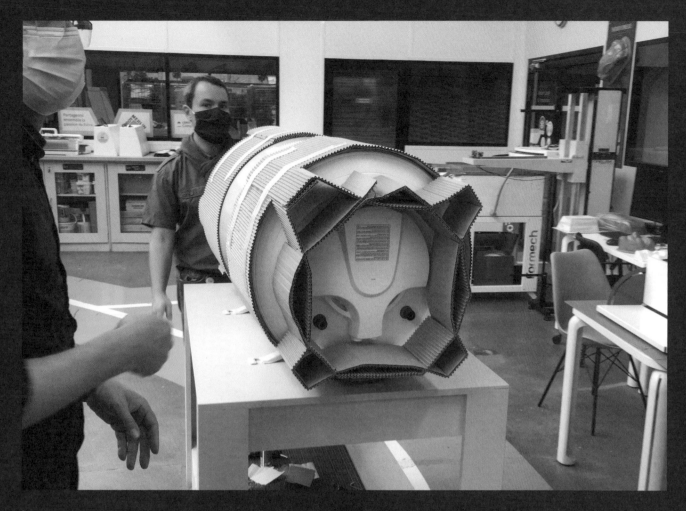

4

4 Enabling companies to make greener choices

IDSL (France)

IDSL x Renault
Understand what electric consumption means in
an electric vehicle. A new visualisation to
understand the impact of actions and to make the
right choices according to the planned route.

IDSL x CITEO
Alternative solution to polystyrene wedging for
CITEO. CITEO is a not-for-profit company with
a view to reduce the environmental impact of
packaging and paper. They help companies find
solutions to their recycling problems, advising
them on environmental responsibility, optimising
low-cost sorting and recycling procedures and
motivating the public to adopt user-friendly
effective sorting.

To bring about meaningful change in communities where people are 'just' trying to survive life's day to day challenges, needs courage, vision and a good dose of imagination. Design fiction is a practice that has the potential to trigger people's inventiveness, even of those who cannot see beyond today's challenges about what should and could be done in the future.

This section addresses the role design fiction must play in challenging environments, as we redesign our futures together. The authors are all working in different continents in peri-urban and rural communities, and for them design fiction is a practice that frames challenges in the context of those most in need, and brings them to the solutioning table as co-solutioneers. The future is up to us all to create.

Design fiction draws you into the space of creating a narrative, and the practice of thinking ahead. It gives birth to powerful ideas and provocations. Not just as an individual flight of fancy, but as an understanding of the future that is co-constructed. Concepts that appeared in science fiction books only a few years ago are now realities in various places.

Finding common ground in Design Fiction

Cal Bruns (Matchboxology, South Africa), Aditya Prakash (Quicksand, India) and José de la O (delaO design studio, Mexico)

The three authors of this essay, Cal, Aditya and José, have experienced the power of applying Design Fiction into practice during many different projects. Although they operate in three different continents, they are all passionate about using Design Fiction as a tool for gathering evidence of solutions that exist today for tomorrow's looming problems. During the conversation they had while writing this essay, they talked about the possibility of making the process of communicating research, and ideas, much more creative, perceptible, and experiential by applying Design Fiction.

Design Fiction is a powerful tactic to challenge preconceptions of what the future might look like. As a structured mindset, it allows one to design for what could (and maybe should) be in our future as opposed to limiting innovation thinking to a specific product or project. Design Fiction brings together diverse teams and unites them in the ability to leapfrog incremental changes and explore disruptive innovations that can create greater impact for desired development outcomes.

Cal As design thinking practitioners, we're constantly breaking down challenges into their human components. We're always reminding our clients that it's not just about what people need, it's what they want that must be front and center in our problem-solving. When I first encountered the Design Fiction concept, I immediately thought — ahh, Science Fiction, a genre of books I've long loved. What captures my imagination in a great SciFi book is not just the possibility of this as a future, but the complexity of the human interactions with it.

Design Fiction parallels this convergence of innovation and humanity. It becomes a powerful tool by gathering accurate and existing evidence of the solutions that exist today for tomorrow's looming problems. It sets up diverse participant groups to connect these clusters of evidence in new and fresh ways to reimagine solutions rooted in probability that better address tomorrow's challenges. It then engages our design expertise to refine those concepts into workable solutions that are practical and desirable; launching them into the public discourse for debate with the goal to inspire more focused innovation.

In this respect it goes a step beyond scenario planning, which is a very popular strategic tool being applied in the private and public sectors today. Once scenario planning evaluates the likelihood of a pool of variables, it sets up a variety of futures which I would characterize as a set of canvasses for Design Fiction to begin to fill in. But as you guys have far more experience applying Design Fiction in practice than I do, why don't you share a few examples of it in action.

Design is a practice that operates jointly with prospective thinking. Designers must anticipate how the products, services, and strategies that are being generated today, are going to be implemented weeks, months, or even years from the first conception. That is why a Designer needs research tools and tactics that could ease this prospective thinking. Furthermore, one of these tactics is a practice known as Design Fiction.

Aditya Thanks Cal. I particularly resonate with the point you make about design fiction providing us the space to set up diverse participant groups to connect clusters of evidence in new and fresh ways. My first introduction to the riches of this process, like I assume for many others, was through the book Speculative Everything, by Dunne and Raby. What particularly excited me, an enthusiastic fiction writer and a novice design researcher, was the possibility of making the process of communicating formal evidence, research, and ideas, much more creative, tactile, perceptible, and experiential.

Another really good example of this is James Chambers' Artificial Defence Mechanisms, a project exploring a simple premise: What if products could protect themselves from threats in their environment the way animals do in nature? Through this, many powerful ideas and provocations around biomimicry, care, connection, and durability are communicated to us, the audience. It is easy to see through this example the perceptibility that this format allows for.

At Quicksand we have been using design fiction mainly for three ends; engaging publics in difficult conversations, helping teams innovate, and helping organisations strategize and reorient. It is always interesting to see the variety of value organisations/clients find in engaging with the process. It helps us too, to discover new opportunities and keep growing our practice.

José I perfectly understand you, Cal: the enthusiasm that you felt the first time you discovered Design Fiction, and probably Aditya, you felt the same, as the three of us are having this conversation. I think the best way to describe how I felt the first time I discovered Design Fiction was pretty similar to the first time I listened to Punk Rock: It challenged my conceptions of the establishment, provoked me, and motivated me to start creating all of this with the right amount of weird. Basically, my brain exploited with the affirmation: IT IS POSSIBLE TO DO THIS!!!

Perhaps one of the most significant Design Fiction attributes and all of those critical and speculative design practices. Is that it not only allows us, designers, to dream beyond the constraints of the market but also could foresee consequences on how society would appropriate these ideas.

One of my favorite examples is James Auger and Anthony Loizeau's 2001 Audio Tooth Implant: A fictional device that promised to receive audio signals on our teeth, transferred via our jaw bone to our inner ear. The result would be a sort of electronic telepathy. Imagine listening to a phone call but without the earplugs. At first hand, this novel idea opens up diverse usability possibilities. Still, while we dive deeper, some darker questions start to emerge. What would it mean for a society to be able to listen without other people's acknowledgment? Would these kinds of devices be illegal?

And that's the beauty of Design Fiction: Designers do not need Design Fiction to think prospectively; we do it already. But sometimes we can be so enclosed in our enthusiasm that we might not see all the possible consequences of our own ideas.

When we talk about design tactics that are, in a way, unconstrained with the commercial aspect of Design, speculation is a method for provocation. Moreover, there is much overlap. As there is Design Fiction, there are other similar practices like Critical Design, Speculative Design, Radical Design, Discursive Design, and a huge etcetera. We are not trying to come up with a full definition, as we prefer to refer to tactics around Design Fiction.

Cal So it's unanimous we embrace Design Fiction as a tool that stretches the value we can bring to our diverse set of clients.

I know Quicksand and Matchboxology are both celebrating 15th year anniversaries this year, and it's safe to say we're both pioneers at fielding human centered design in peri-urban and rural communities, where people are just trying to survive life's day to day challenges. Not sure about India and Latin America, but across Africa we often encounter the "one day is one day" survival philosophy; where people in really tough life situations just focus on making today the best it can be because they see very little opportunity to make tomorrow any different.

I think this poses an interesting question to who participates in design fiction exercises.

We've all found techniques and methodologies that unlock the problem solving genius in otherwise very ordinary people. One of the most successful techniques we employ in our work in Africa is asking workshop problem-solvers to imagine they are suddenly in charge of solving a specific problem, and have to report back why their solution was a raging success to the President of the country.

I'm wondering if this isn't a simplistic form of design fiction with a bit of concrete reality thrown in to help make it easier to engage people who ordinarily don't think much beyond the following day? What do you guys think? Can you share some details of how you've successfully fielded design diction in your own practices and what sorts of results you generated?

Ideas that are generated by Design fiction, can come from a lot of places and end up going to a few different others. This mode of storytelling allows an exploration into the world as it is seen and experienced, and poses a set of simple questions—what can become of this, and what can we learn from this becoming?

Aditya For me, a really interesting trajectory of engagements in this space of futuring began with HUM.2035, a project exploring the future of humanitarian work in South Asia. This project was initially commissioned by the Barbican Center in London. We were to design an exhibit for their Life Rewired Hub—a pop-up space that engages with the 'dizzying' impact of technological and scientific change; questioning what it means to be human today. This commision rode on the back of the work of our partners Tandem Research, and the work we had been doing with the Humanitarian Leadership Academy. Our brief was to engage audiences in a conversation around the future of humanitarian work, and the role of technology within. We called this project, 'HUM', as it was both a short form for Humanitarian, and it also means 'us', or 'we', in Hindi.

This was exciting because we were presented with the opportunity to elevate the research we conduct into a built-world of the future, with communities, ecosystems, personas, artefacts, crises, and so on. We could communicate emerging trends and best practices driving the humanitarian sector by applying them onto the lives of fictional stakeholders: communities, families, and citizens, one journey at a time, and see how those take form in future times of crises, mapping their needs, expectations, and systems of resilience!

The process we followed was somewhat as follows (ofcourse, all this becomes only much clearer in retrospect):

1. Investigate
Scanning the humanitarian ecosystem and its various tenets. We focused on forms of aid, prevalent crises in South Asia, innovation, unmet needs, and gaps. The knowledge we uncovered fell into the following buckets: Climate Tensions, Technology and a Push Towards a Digital Present, and Humanitarian Siloes and Local Networks of Care

2. Speculate
Narrowing down and building over our findings and imagining worlds and spaces where they are allowed to evolve and disintegrate, in internal and external workshop settings. This is an example of a storytelling template we used in workshops to develop early ideas of personas in the worlds we built:

TELLING THE STORY OF _____
TRYING TO _____
IN A WORLD WHERE _____

As interesting and engaging Design Fiction might be, one should approach Design Fiction with caution. Contrary to other Design practices, like Human Centered Design or Design Thinking, Design fiction does not have a clear methodology that could help us reach successful results. As any creative tactic, the person deploying it has to have a critical approach and constant realisation on the limitations of the idea being generated.

3. Curate
Coming to terms with the world we want to build; the story we want to tell. What are the key themes we want to highlight (and hence evolve into the future)? What are the crises we want to base it around?

4. Create
Producing the story to be communicated. This included personas, 360 illustrations, virtual spaces, print media, physical artefacts, and videos.

The project was very well received, we were successful generating thought and provoking conversations, and it led to an extremely interesting line of further engagements. But before continuing to ramble along, José, do you want to share some of your work?

HUM.2035 — Speculations into the future of humanitarian work in South Asia

Told from the perspective of HUM, a fictional humanitarian aid network founded in 2020 India, the project, first displayed at the Life Rewired Hub in London, tells the stories of HUM-affiliated humanitarian workers dealing with the aftermath of storm Lata which has recently hit Goa. In it are explored themes like the purpose of upskilling and questions around employment when facing displacement, the use of mobile-based or digital services, encouraging multidisciplinarity across sectors (from food provision to health care to financial inclusion) and the support of local efforts and knowledge.

These visuals show the humanitarian heroes that come together to help revitalise communities and make them more resilient.

Clockwise from top left:

FED Farmers — Displaced farmers, engineers and botanists in collaboration with the FEDs, are working day and night in pop-up experimental growing labs to tend to the high demand of locally grown food post the floods

MED.CN epidemiologists — Given the lack of prompt response the last time the city was affected by an epidemic, MED.CN put together a team of trained personnel (Biologists, Epidemiologists and Public health workers) ready to confront and contain an epidemic quickly, to study outbreaks, and setup an immediate system of response; from disease surveillance to coordinated treatment

Med.CN health workers — The role of MED.CN health workers is to provide adapted care to affected communities, namely via telemedicine services on hand-held tablets carried by WHEL staff for initial check-ups

The informal engineer — After realizing the vulnerabilities in his informal community in South Goa, and state inaction to recognize the settlement and equitably provide it with public resources, this engineer has taken it upon himself to learn, and train others in his (and other) community(s) on how the power of local resources, e-waste, and renewable energy can be harnessed to generate quick and resilient solutions.

José Of course, Aditya. I'm a frequent participant on various global initiatives that promote Speculative Design and a shared conversation is how the future should be more democratic. Like you describe Cal, here in México, immediacy is a crucial issue that does not allow people to think ahead on every social level. We have been collaborating with some companies and institutions on finding ways to talk about democratic futures.

One example is a project we participated in with the bank BBVA and Centro University. We designed what in Design Fiction is called Diegetic Prototypes for different future scenarios related to banking. A diegetic prototype is a fictional product that helps carry the narrative for a specific scenario, like a prop from an alternative reality. As four different scenarios were presented to us, A trending future scenario (where things continue business as usual), a utopian scenario, a catastrophic future and lastly, what we call a "Futurible" scenario, where is a desirable future.

We designed four different objects for each scenario or parallel reality that showed how society would do finance. This project was a fantastic opportunity to analyze our own culture on how things were built, and how "product development" would look like in each parallel reality. As these kinds of exercises work as conversational pieces, we speculate what variety of materials, tools, and technology these near-future scenarios would be available and start designing and building these prototypes. For this type of exercise, each device should also speak on the communities' dreams and frustrations in these societies in a more engaging way. These prototypes are intended to serve as tools for debate with critical decision-makers as a way for them to explore not so obvious consequences of what the bank is planning for the future.

Another project that is very close to my heart is not a commission but an academic project. RoboKumbia is a semester-long project that I developed with a group of Industrial Design senior students to answer the question: How would technology look like if it was entirely conceived in México? One of the great things that Design Fiction has put on the table is to bring the aspirational side of how technology should look like. Science Fiction has indeed motivated designers and engineers into bringing innovation. Still, it has brought a western-centric aesthetic in technology. Some exercises of Design Fiction challenges these conceptions and bring other voices to the table. Afrofuturism is a great example.

So, to answer the question of how Mexican Technology would look like, the students designed a Cumbia-Playing robotic orchestra. Each robot was inspired by urban elements that the students found around them, from food markets to public transport. This type of project's importance is to let (in this case, design students) realize that technology can be closer to our own culture, without the clichés and post-colonial aspirations, bringing a new true identity on how we can shape our future.

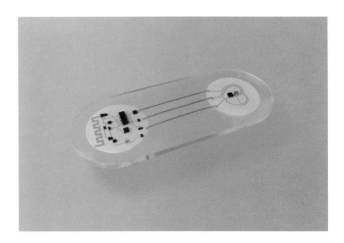

Subcutaneous Biometric Sensor. This Diegetic prototype was commissioned by BBVA and Centro University to visualize the Utopic Future Scenario, in which banks uses biometric subcutaneous devices to offer more personalized services depending on the information captured by the biometric implant.

Robokumbia. is an Academic Project designed by industrial students from Monterrey Institute of Technology in the Mexico City Region and directed by Studio José de la O. The objective of the project is to speculate how technology would look like if it's conceived on a Mexican-Urban context.

Aditya Sorry for cutting in line, Cal. Wanted to wrap up speaking about our projects before we move on :)

Our HUM exhibition at the Barbican Center in London was successful in positioning our design fiction practice globally, and it was received with intrigue and enthusiasm. Members from the innovation team of MSF (Médecins Sans Frontières / Doctors Without Borders) had visited our exhibit, and were very interested in the process we used, and the stories we told. This led to a series of successful projects with MSF, with the objective of not only exploring the space of design fiction within the formal systems of the organization, but also using design fiction as a tool to imagine alternative futures for MSF, and use those as starting points for conversations on organizational change. Through these engagements we learnt a lot about the value of design fiction within humanitarian spaces — which tend to be short-term, and responsive.

On the back of this, and a talk by Avinash at the Primer conference, me and Rohan, a colleague from Quicksand, applied for the Next Generation Foresight Practitioners award. We were awarded the Asia Special Award, recognising not just the value of our projects in this space, but also encouraging us to take this practice forward — to new explorations and collaborations.

Experiences like these reaffirm my belief in design fiction as a process that can immensely further the world of design research, and the strides it can take to communicate research findings, bring people/ teams together, initiate difficult conversations, build speculative worlds, and experience preferable futures.

As Design Fiction relies on narrative, the designer has to find the right balance for the strangeness this reality might have. Use too little fiction, the narrative will be too close to home, hence, boring and not provoking. Use too much fiction, fantasy and exaggerations, and the concept might be way too strange for the audience and they will dismiss the concept.

Cal Impressive body of work guys! In Africa we're seeing important innovations that highlight the relevance and immediate potential impact of this design fiction way of thinking.

As you may know, Cape Town suffered a sudden and extreme draught two years ago and we were within a few weeks away of Day ZERO — the day in which the taps of our 1.5 million citizens would run dry. A solution waiting in the wings were two self-contained mobile desalination superbarges from Saudi Arabia, able to immediately sail down and begin generating 50,000 cubic meters of fresh water to residents every day.

In healthcare, concepts that appeared in science fiction books only a few years ago are now realities on the African continent. Drones are delivering lifesaving medical supplies to rural clinics and doctors in Ghana, Tanzania and Rwanda. Villages that were nearly impossible to get to in the rainy seasons are now served by Zipline; a San Francisco based medical delivery company. The scarcity of physicians on the African continent is being addressed in ingenious ways. Osgenic, a Finnish company, is revolutionizing the way surgeons can be trained remotely via virtual reality. HIghly experienced doctors from around the world are able to improve the continent's healthcare thanks to breakthroughs in telemedicine. Hospitals in Ethiopia are now sending locally generated patient scans in real time to oncological radiologists in the US and UK for better diagnoses.

Agricultural innovations are also exploding across the continent to address food scarcity. Drone mapping helps agri-scientists better support small scale farmers with crop health & maturity. Mobile apps are connecting small farmers to markets more efficiently, improving their viability as suppliers to regular buyers and increasing their revenue. Innovations like GrowBox, a company that retrofits old shipping containers to be portable indoor grow rooms suddenly make farming on rooftops in urban slum areas a possibility.

While I've shown you the future is here, I do one critically important role design fiction must play as we redesign our futures. It's critical that we frame community and continent challenges in the context of those most in need and bring them to the solutioning table as co-solutioneers. Innovations are only impactful if they are implemented. People in resource scarce environments are experts at generating hacks and workarounds because their survival depends on it. By including them into the design fiction process, we not only harness their ingenuity and creativity, we integrate their perspectives and realities into the problem statements. In doing so, we have the ability to not just envision better futures but to ensure they can come to be.

Let us look at one particular project in this space that illustrates this; James Chambers' Artificial Defense Mechanisms'. He explores a simple question:

What if products could protect themselves from threats in their environment the way animals do in nature? Would we take better care of them? Would they last longer? Would we feel sorry for them?

This led to the creation of three prototypes: FLOPPY LEGS (a portable hard drive that 'stands up' when it senses water nearby, THE GESUNDHEIT RADIO (a radio that 'sneezes' periodically to remove settling dust that could cause it to malfunction) , and the ANTITOUCH LAMP (a lamp with a hot halogen bulb that 'sways' away when it senses someone nearby). What really stands out is how mere objects have been personified via actions given to them; like that of standing up, sneezing, swaying.

The Gesundheit Radio. A radio sits on a shelf, gathering dust. If it goes unused for a long period of time, the dust can ultimately cause it to stop working. The Gesundhiet Radio solves this problem by periodically cleaning itself with a mechanical 'sneeze' (the sneeze can also be triggered manually)

Although its original source is unknown, this proposal for an airport built over skyscrapers in a city is a good example of how the field of architecture and urban planning makes use of speculation to start thinking about complex problems—in this case locating airports in the hearts of congested cities, or more broadly, growing cities and mobility within them.

Proposes Orientable Roof-Top Airports For Cities

PROPOSED as a solution to the problem of locating an airport in the heart of any big city, a design for a long orientable run- way, which would be mounted on circular tracks atop tall buildings, as sketched above, has been conceived by a French engineer.

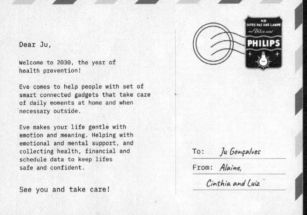

1

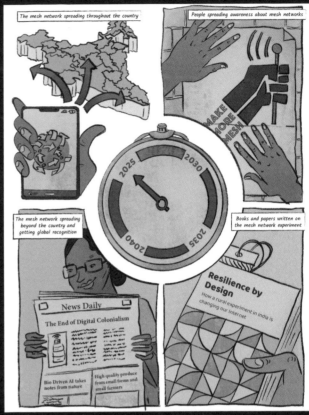

2

1 Postcards from the future

Flutter Innovation (Brazil)

What does the future of healthcare look like for populations across the globe, and how do you believe tech will influence design for healthcare? Postcards from the future is a workshop that Flutter Innovation is doing for more than 10 years for Philips Design Brazil. Flutter Innovation invites people working for Philips Brazil to send themselves a postcard from the future.

2 Hopeful Futures

Quicksand (India)

Quicksand's project with the University of Dundee to co-create new narratives for decentralised digital futures with rural communities in Karnataka, India. Our attempt was to challenge existing narratives, telling new stories that reflect the diverse hopes that people from rural areas have for their futures and the roles that emerging technologies might play in supporting these. We called these Hopeful Futures. And we explored these through stories as bridges that can connect communities, engage stakeholders and inform policy makers.

3

3 The future of community health

Matchboxology (South Africa)

Reinventing South African communities without HIV was a beautiful use of design fiction as a methodology. We challenged teams to reinvent community health workers as a profession and equip them with tools and backpacks that gave them the ability to amplify the breakthroughs we know are coming through in the next decade from big pharma.

4 Open-ended objects

IDSL (France)

To kick-off projects, we design mediums such as probes, 'experiential shots', immersive environments, etc. These help participants to get inspired, to understand issues, deflect from their own expertise, immerse themselves as close as possible to real contexts to tackle problems more easily and quickly. One of the probes translated a technological asset created by the R&D department into an open object, allowing multi-disciplinary participants to understand what the asset does and come up with new use cases (e.g. making the haptic and multitouch surface vibrate more as you stroke the surface). Two brainstormings sessions used cardboard and paper to contextualize ideas and build new experiences. A quick and inexpensive open installation option allowed anyone (without technical expertises) to come up with solutions for poly-sensorial experiences (sound, light, smell, etc) in a car cockpit.

4

Future Probing

**Exploring possible futures together
to gain tangible benefits already today**

5

5 Future Probing on dolphins, and bats

Summ()n (Russia & Netherlands)

Already for years we use the metaphor of dolphins to explain the logic of the Summ()n Future Probing method (the creature has become the mascot of the team in many ways). Dolphins are smart, social, playful - there are a lot of 'positive' qualities in these animals. Similar to people, dolphins have five senses - e.g., then can see, hear, smell etc. However, unlike people the dolphins have an additional sense: their sonar allows them to emit sound waves that quickly travel through water, bounce off any objects near them, and come back to dolphins with the useful information about what's ahead. We consistently say that we are on a mission to 'doplhinize' our clients, by training them to probe the emerging social space around them by developing - and testing - multiple future probes. PS: During 2020 we increasingly used another metaphor: the bats. Coincidentally,

these creatures have quite similar echolocation capacities. Perhaps not so coincidentally, they are much less popular in cultures (and this unpopularity sharply increased lately). Future Probing can - and should - learn from the bats, too. Too many of these 'speculative designs' develop very optimistic, wishful-thinking types of futures, and have a peculiar blind spot to the dark forces at play. And no, developing simple black and white, utopia-dystopia dichotomies is not a remedy for these blind spots.

Play

Heraclitus, the Greek philosopher once said: "Change is the only constant in life." However, success in bringing meaningful change is never guaranteed. In fact, change is often met with resistance. Whether it comes to physiological barriers, or resistance as a socio-cultural phenomenon, a research or design consultant should be ready to face the multiple forms of resistance that can come up during projects and to eventually 'play' with it.

It is popular to read about research and design projects that inspire by example. Either the method or the outcome is held up as a grand lesson. But there are no easy lessons in the space of resistance. How for instance can a service be of service when the paying client (team) resists all forms of collaboration? By unpacking differing encounters with clients, we are able to witness the 'social designs' that clients may have for resisting an advisor which they have hired.

Designers cannot base their model of the world on the world that they wish for. It would amount to projecting our values and judgments onto the lives of others. However, it requires emotional strength to withstand difficult encounters. Design is considered as a 'social construct' in this section. After all, workshop-participants are designing forms of resistance and improvising as the workshop program emerges. Resistances have a right to exist. How hard they may be. It is our job to deal with it and to break through resistance-patterns. Sometimes the best way to deal with it is playfully.

Making sense of resistance

Michael Davis-Burchat (Big Human, Canada), and Slava Kozlov & Katerina Khomenchuk (Summ( )n Futures, Russia and Netherlands)

Success is never guaranteed for a consultant, even if it's the first thing that a client wants to hear about from an external advisor. The very meaning of 'success' is debatable in our field, in fact the difference in interpretations of 'success' is one of the major difficulties in our work.

In 1915, Arthur D. Little pioneered the modern idea of consulting, as a way to offer businesses safe passage into unknown territory. A century later, consulting services are more familiar now. It is popular to oversimplify consulting as some sort of request for a result — often called a deliverable. Which is not the most helpful notion to hang on to. Maybe this is a good time to search for a better label for our work practice? And maybe we can get better at discussing how an agent conducts themselves as *the outsider*? Either way, we find it revealing to look at resistance, as expressed during the dance that goes

on between a *client* and its *agent*.

Anyone that can remain elastic about who they are and who they wish to become will lean into situations of change. Those wishing to maintain order as it is, will find it in themselves to resist.

This text offers a tale of two differing encounters with clients. Experiences that are admittedly told from the bias of the specific agency who encountered it. We wouldn't expect to describe the fullness of this subject in a single comparison, so we invite you to compare your own experiences to the pair that we report on here. It is our plan to expand on this subject for some time to come. And to learn from the stories that readers share with us. As you read further you may want to stir in some memories of your own. The purpose of this text is to share why we get excited by the fullness of complex topics. And to broaden an awareness about the social arrangements which inevitably surround the client, the agent and their work.

On occasion, companies require outside expertise to refresh their collective imagination. Once we demonstrate the nature and relevance of our know-how, that practice gets treated with respect by the person who hires us on. Usually, our contract (their seal of approval) spreads quickly to anyone else in the firm that we engage with. The comparison you are about to read will straddle two types of relationships. In the Summ()n example the social agreement is widely accepted. However in the Big Human example the contract breaks down; as professional norms erode and rudeness takes over the social situation.

A feature shared in these examples, and also wider across other projects we work on, focuses on changing people (or helping people to change themselves.) Each instance can vary in the degree of change on offer. In some cases change is minor; learning some new facts, figures or techniques. More deeply it can involve changing attitudes, ideas, or patterns of behavior. Resistance to change will take on many more forms. We offer our two accounts to share and look closely at.

In the Summ()n Futures encounter, people within the client team may balk at using their imagination with new freedoms. A mental model, a sense of identity, or a particular attitude are some of the hidden forces that can limit one's scope of imagination. By extension, one can view any subject narrowly, through a single lens. The urge to oversimplify one's understanding *of the world* will make it impossible to hold two — or many more — competing ideas in mind at once. To a *coach* or a *guide*, such hidden forces reveal themself as resistance within the mind of the beholder.

In the Big Human encounter, people within the client team express their resistance divisively. Making it clear that they had never accepted the contract that was established (ostensibly) on their behalf. In this social situation a wide range of signs and symbols had been used to promote a company wide *change initiative*. That is to say every employee was invited to participate in a grand adventure. A troubling confluence of labels, messages, and processes all played a role in revealing resistances within the social structure of the company. As well as the emotional center of many individuals involved.

We report on the world with a first person account of things we want to understand. Doing so, will raise eyebrows about bias, and ontological conflicts that show up *when describing the world as we experience it*. This defect occurs naturally, no matter which words we choose. We do not claim that these reports alone can represent the subject of resistance in its entirety. Still, there is plenty here to think about in greater depth as we examine surprising ways that resistance emerges, and what its appearances are trying to say to us.

An unwelcoming experience

To wade into still waters is to experience relief, yet the very same waters will feel frightening when the current picks up, where a river begins to narrow. Trouble can find us in the plainest encounters. Work environments offer their own dangers. Psychological safety may be something we come to expect in the professional world. So what is an advisor to do when the people you are serving behave more rudely than any group you have worked with before?

Big Human had been hired to a dream project. A long standing client CEO asked us to help innovate the service culture of his whole company. That would involve working with everyone. And it meant modernizing their relationship to the people who line up in the lobby for service. Within minutes of getting started, we could tell that the dreamyness of the project wasn't going to last.

Consulting works well when outsiders are welcomed into an alliance, to work as partners. In business publications 'client resistance' is seen as a negative force that can be detected early, understood, and counteracted. Peter Block offers this comment, that "Resistance is a predictable, natural reaction against the process of being helped." In this line of reason not only should the agent take this for granted. They must know in advance ways to counteract every disruption to their work.

Indeed, resistance can be seen as a desired reaction of any healthy organism (or organization) to the external impact (whether helpful or harmful). For instance, we praise successful defense mechanisms of our immune system when they protect us against the damage that can be brought on by malignant bacteria. This dilemma would come into focus, when we normally make introductions and establish trust.

How does one distinguish when change will be good, versus something to push back on? Particularly at the beginning of a three month engagement? After all, Big Human is in the business of *helping*. A related question emerges; how does any *consultant* succeed when engaging a defiant host? It would be cynical for them to pay for work that is designed to fail.

Deciding on the why of things

When we engage clients, we tend to focus more on *The why of things* than *The how of things*. Instead of providing ready-made solutions or processes, we participate in the creation of new knowledge and new ways of interpreting familiar situations. Our work better resembles 'coaching' than 'consulting', and even more specifically, often looks like the role of 'playing coach'.

Interestingly, this type of delivery can trigger its own range of complaints. In many cases clients, at least initially, have come to think of designers as *the answer people*. The entire reason for a human centered approach is to reveal real opportunities for growth. We pass on an interest into mundane things, using a beginner's mind and a sunny imagination. That makes us act more like *the question people*.

The place for civility in transformation

It is natural for an individual to think impartially. It is also natural for individuals to be aware of a consensus interpretation. In a workplace, some will speak freely about, and navigate differing viewpoints. Others will feel insecure about raising their voice.

In some organizations it can feel unsafe to speak up without damaging your career path. It is axiomatic that freedom of thought is the fuel of creativity. So, the fear of speaking up will cast a chill on things. Cognitive resistance can help us look at something from multiple points of view. Whereas social violence will cause your collaborators to withdraw. Aesop pictured this phenomenon with his parable about the cloud challenging the sun to a friendly competition.

Multicultural environments further complicate the work of sensemaking and interpretation. As there are more lenses available to interpret facts with. Resistance shows up differently in different cultures and is not limited to a predefined list of behaviors. Distinctly new types of resistance keep shifting all the time. So it is impossible to anticipate all of the ways to counteract resistance. Or how to know when an act of defiance might just make things better for the whole group.

Transformations require people and organizations to let go one philosophy, in exchange for a new one. Civil discourse helps smooth the way forward.

For now though, let's look into a story of revolt. And to displays of defiance that met Big Human in a workshop for 35 people.

What a standoff reveals
On this particular morning, we spent an hour arranging a conference room. Tables are covered with sharpies, post-it notes and a learning agenda. The moment before a workshop gathers usually fills us with jitters. Until we sense a social connection forming, our minds dart around, looking for tiniest detail that can dampen an otherwise generative experience.

Everything seems in place. We feel excited as we welcome our audience and get to know people by name and role. Soon enough though, the experience feels unusually dark. Our every attempt to lighten the mood is met with snark or reprisal. Our first hour together casts shade on us and

our motives. Courtesy, it seems, is on vacation and we still have a three month program ahead of us. This level of revolt has never happened to us before.

It is never simple to align with the collective imagination of others. Organizations apply boundaries to the imagination using factors like seniority, role, and business activity. Boundaries help decide who will reason about what, unfortunately they overlook how people feel about things and have their voices heard. Work values, personal goals, education, and other cultural markers create implicit channels of affinity that org. charts and strategic plans never will.

What has become clear in this example is that consulting is never based on a two party relationship — client side, and service side. There is always at least one more party involved. In our example we think of them as *the audience*. The project we were hired to do was internally facing, making it applicable to every member of the organization. In our case we were blindsided by the illusion of agreement.

Therapists refer to a list of the many kinds of resistances they face in their work. All of which fall into four buckets; arguing, interrupting, denying and ignoring. In this particular engagement all of them were getting put to use to get our attention and our respect. Incivility we should note may come from all three entities in the social/political relationship. Anthropologist, David Graeber, explained that a three party relationship makes things ripe for bullying to take place.

What felt heartbreaking about the social divide, was that the rudest members of our audience had worked amicably with us before. In fact they had co-designed the goal for this project — during a previous project. Further to the point, they had once pleaded with us to make this goal come true. So how can we explain their efforts to thwart things?

And if they weren't willing to engage with us in the workshop, at this juncture, how was any transformation supposed to happen?

Trigger words
A political dynamic that had popped up between the two projects was this emerging sense that *management* was not treating *labour* respectfully. Applying yet another layer of division to the social dynamic of the company. And making it

hard for many employees to invest in practicing a future way of getting along.

As we unpacked our tools and described the new project, trigger words revealed symptoms of discord about political arrangements. Our client relationship reported directly to the Chief Executive. To ensure that all employees of the company could participate in our '*journey project*', he chose "make it mandatory". To ensure that *journey* was sufficiently funded. And to hold us publicly accountable '*journey*' was designed as a "training program".

If I can ask you to stand in the shoes of the rebellious ones for the moment, you will notice the word *mandatory* can mean someone has taken your autonomy from you — and you might want that back. And secondly, you notice that *training program* can suggest that your competence is lacking somehow. A notion will never feel welcome.

Having kicked the hornet's nest was one thing. We would be treated unfriendly early and often. But we had recovered from incivility often enough before. Just never so fierce or incessantly. We could provide some gentle forms of therapy, but the clock was ticking and we weren't getting any work done. Not ours, nor theirs.

Looking back now, we needed to be more explicit that we were the third party to the relationship. Rather than the secret agent of an adversary. Just honest in our role as coaches. We were most surprised when the audience didn't receive this whole effort as a way to difficult situation, a whole lot better. Our repeated explanations fell flat.

We could imagine representing the needs of the disempowered but how to help them now when their every effort was to remain helpless? Why isn't there a robust *theory of rudeness* about the workplace that might help us decode the attacks we faced? Why do business journals provide so little help in this space? Lost in the gap between our consulting team and the audience was an emancipating idea that we were there to bring into being.

Following a gloomy meeting with the chief executive, we would resolve to press on. From where we stood, project-failure was clearly in view. Neither he nor us looked forward to that result.

"No one has said why we are doing this? Nothing is going to change until the management changes first? ... And, who are you to say we don't use empathy in our work, and what are you trying to [imply] about us? Participant in 'journey project'

Still, neither of us could imagine a work around that was capable of thawing the resistance we faced. If our chances looked slim, our shared vision for a more caring workplace was dropping from sight as well.

Showing before telling
A workable peace with our audience was reached the next day. Even if it didn't come with a sense of alacrity, we were still swimming in the same waters. We went about modeling different ways to engage in acts of decision making, from the bottom of the hierarchy on up.

Axiomatically, it is hard to grow when one chooses contempt over a sunny disposition of curiosity. Disengagement also has a demoralizing effect on teammates who would prefer to opt try something new. With most of our audience working to rule, we spent most of our time building trust. And some of it is looking for a key that might open a different relationship. The whole arrangement set the journey project on a downward spiral. No amount of reasoning seemed to release the undercurrent of resistance.

It didn't feel reasonable that our audience disowned something they had so openly cherished. The choice to be rude, was winning out over self interest. Acts of defiance seemed more important now than making things better.

On closer study, rudeness in the workplace is represented by papers which say in effect that more study of

impoliteness will be needed before we can form a robust theory. We would not win by reasoning with the unreasonable. The trick was to engage using a different center of mind where *mirror neurons* do their work.

Mirror neurons allow people to learn through imitation. They enable us to mimic body language, or even an athlete's fine-motor skill. What made them relevant to this situation is how they also enable people to *feel the emotions of others*. And they act as if on autopilot. By mirroring the actions of others we understand people *not by thinking but by feeling*. Could they help us in our hour of darkness?

Armed with this knowledge we changed course from telling to showing. It would require us to throw out the thinking tools we had invested so much time in creating. Rather than explaining a thought process, we would now take 40 minutes to *perform* the work, as it were. In effect, we were now showing something rather than teaching about it.

Our social relations did not suddenly become any stronger. Luckily for everyone they didn't need to be. The practice of mimicry let our audience think appreciatively. And on their own terms. Something that was impossible when we tried to reason, felt natural when they were allowed to *feel something* in advance of reasoning.

Soon the teams in our audience were grasping concepts and asking about nuances without any prompts from us.

Reflections on the 'journey project' and resistance
Our client believed that the 'journey project' was a wildly ambitious goal before we started. Still, we found it adventurous to take because each party thought like activists about making work better for every employee of the firm. What we hadn't expected was how unwelcome the adventure would prove to be.

With two more workshops this project would engage every employee and every manager in the organization. By the time our project had ended 8 out of 12 projects were considered successful — by the whole organization — because they originated from the bottom up. And culturally speaking over 42% of the people would opt in,

to a more caring disposition of service. Which was more than double the rate that we had hoped for! Employees that were once hostile would openly admit to feeling renewed by the project. And excited by a new sense of agency and empowerment.

As outsiders, our behaviors will take cues from the host that hires us. If they ask us to be serious we will become more businesslike. Yet we are reminded in telling these stories that creativity relies on two habits. Playfulness, and mimicry. Remaining playful in the most serious of engagements allows one to think without an invisible layer of censorship. Roleplay finds the most direct path up a mountainous climb. And mimicry offers the most direct way to understand the meaning of things. Because the meaning of work is in the mind of the audience, and not the consultant.

Looking back on *the journey*, it was the resistance we faced that taught us new lessons. About how cultural shifts ought to happen. Without anyone losing face during the process of transformation.

"Why does our culture need to change? ...This is just another binder full of shit that I will throw in the garbage when you leave this room. Who are you to tell us that we should be better at our jobs? What are you really trying to say about us? Why are you trying to teach us empathy when we ... could teach you about empathy?"
Participant in 'journey project'

Playfulness as a Method to Overcome Cognitive Inertia

What are the 'Futures Complex' (and why are they resisted)?

In our practice at Summ()n Futures we encounter many of the resistance-prone interactions between clients and consultants that are discussed in the introduction to this text. However, some of the challenges that we regularly face are somewhat different and very specific to our work. We relate them to the notorious notion of 'futures'.

It has been often portrayed (and perceived as such by our clients) that the main problem in dealing with the 'futures' is our capacity to predict them, both accurately and well-ahead. As an example of such an attitude we refer to the title of the recently published book by William Poundstone, 'How to Predict Everything'. This attitude typically manifests in our clients' requests that may sound like "Can you predict what will happen in 2030? And in 2050?"

Our professional expertise (and also life-long experience by now) indicates that the main, and much more sinister problem lies not in our inability to foresee certain future developments, but in our unstoppable tendency to project current state of affairs, current social fabric into the future. We are happy to accept colorful 'future visions' peppered with the latest and edgiest technologies – provided that they remain stunningly similar to our world today. "The future will have flying cars, yes – but otherwise be just like the now" could be a good summary of such an approach.

The above description could be seen as too abstract and too exaggerated. To make it more tangible and concrete, let's consider a specific example. This example is borrowed from the project called En L'An 2000 ('In the year 2000') created around the 1900-s by the French artist Jean-Marc Côté. In his project Jean-Marc Côté tried to envision life in Europe in the year 2000; in other words, in one hundred years

further from his present situation (using contemporary professional slang we could describe this project as a case of 'speculative design.')

After consultations with scientists and experts from different fields, he created more than sixty 'future vignettes', drawings that illustrated various aspects of life in that future. Below is just one example of his drawings, in this case presenting the future of education, or more specifically, a 'classroom in the year 2000':

The scene is centered around an unnamed apparat, a book processor of a kind. This device transforms books into electric signals that are sent directly to the brains of the pupils. The role of the teacher is to merely feed this machine with the books.

Today we can smile at this vision (or could feel envy at this possibility, depending on our take on the purpose of education). In any case, we will likely all agree that this was not a very accurate 'forecast': the classrooms in the year 2000 did not look like the one in this picture.

However, we are also aware that in the last hundred years researchers made a colossal progress in our understanding of how the brain works. There is an ever-growing interest to the brain-to-computer, computer-to-brain and even brain-to-brain technologies. The most recent example of Neuralink Corporation founded by Elon Musk is just another confirmation of the desire (of at least some people) to make this picture a reality, one day. Maybe this 'future classroom' prediction was just a bit too early?

At the same time, and if we don't interpret the picture too literally, we may say that such a future is already here. The students today listen to audiobooks through their headsets in almost exactly the same manner today. Such things as 'audio courses' have already been used in education for decades, and today you might expect to see in modern classrooms much more exotic things like 'immersive VR goggles'. In other words, this depiction of the future could just as well be a very accurate one.

Having discussed these pro-s and con-s, we can also invite the reader to look at the same picture again, and try to see something very strange in it, something that could be seen as

scandalous and almost insulting to us today. When presenting this story in different audiences, we usually give people a chance to comment on this picture. As a rule, it is a female voice that points out One Big Issue with this picture: There are only boys in this class.

We can obviously understand how this happened: There were only boys in the French classes in the year 1900 (or perhaps more accurately, there were separate classes for boys and girls at this time). Girls had much simpler, and shorter school programs, and women were not allowed to enter higher education colleges or universities. Having such social context as a 'norm of life' around him, Jean-Marc Côté simply projected this 'reality' into the very distant future he tried to portray.

It is easy to critique this future visioning as naïve and unsophisticated, and the practice of the past. However, and unfortunately way too often we see very similar patterns in our very contemporary projects, too. Our customers eagerly project the current status quo as possible futures.

We call these projections 'Futures Simple' and juxtapose them to 'Futures Complex', more complex (sic!) representations of the possible futures, developed on the premises that many of our contemporary social norms and practices may change significantly in that future.

Not surprisingly, such complex futures are difficult to produce. They require in-depth understanding of today's realities and at the same time attention to the emerging changes of these realities, capacity to sense the 'signals of the future'. Even when produced, these Futures Complex are more difficult to believe in and these possible future scenarios are often met with skepticism. Most importantly, the ideas about different 'strange' futures rarely motivate people to start changing their established practices today.

In other words, when we try to help people to deal with these Future Complex, we face numerous 'resistances', and on different levels. Some of these resistances are cognitive and rational: it is not easy to spot certain underlying assumptions behind our dominant worldview and even more difficult to imagine possible alternatives.

Other types of resistances are more social and even political in nature: Many of our contemporary practices and norms have active supporters, with multiple vested interests, and these people don't want to change their beliefs and behavior easily, whether on a personal, corporate, or societal level.

The status quo can be legitimized in form of written laws or exist as unspoken but powerful corporate cultures or social etiquettes. Whatever the form, these existing powers don't like to be challenged. Of course, our internal personal reluctance to change plays a big role in this 'resistance cocktail', too.

Why do we play with the futures?

How do we deal with such resistances? As already mentioned in the introduction, one of the first rules is to admit that these resistances have a right to exist. We don't blame people for having and expressing them. Rather, we seek for the meaningful and responsible ways to help them to become aware of their own resistance patterns and look for alternative, more complex ideas (about the futures, in this case.)

We often present 'playfulness' as an essential quality of our practice in general. This quality is expressed in the very motto of Summ( )n: 'We summon the futures to play with them now'. It is also embedded in the specific tools and methods that we use (such as Future Probing method).

Being playful for us does not mean to just 'have fun', or to apply a few common (often fairly manipulative) tricks popularized by some 'gamification' practitioners. We see playfulness as a vehicle, an enabler that could help people to be different and to imagine/ create alternatives, even if only in a 'magical circle' of game in the beginning.

Being different and acting from a different position ('role') can sensitize people to the very possibility of such differences. Eventually it also helps them in creating very different ideas and artifacts for these alterative and more complex futures. An opportunity to see other people playing different roles and empathically reflecting on the achieved results is another powerful quality of this approach.

The exact applications of this method, the 'gameplays' that we develop and use, vary and depend on specific

Classroom of the year 2000

contexts, including project related specifics and general social and cultural factors.

In some cases we employ very overt, explicit game-like settings and rules. For example, during a workshop we facilitated at the GOOD19 conference in London, we suggested to enact very stereotypical, almost caricature roles, such as Elves or Dwarfs. The teams had to develop their concepts for the future from these imaginary identities.

In many other cases, the qualities of playfulness that we apply are much more subtle, yet nevertheless prominent. For instance, during our Future Probing process, itself quite complex and multi-staged, we have a specific activity when we build the 'worlds of the future'.

These worlds are not just 'what if' fantastic scenarios. Their initial grounding insights come from the analysis of multiple 'signals of the future', and collaborative efforts to make sense of them. In any case, these world-building exercises always call for imagination, creativity, and creative story-telling.

We ask participants to literally construct imaginary 'future worlds' where certain qualities — the ones that may look strange and unusual today — become the new norm, manifest everywhere and impact all aspects of life.

We support this activity by providing creative building kits and other tools to facilitate this demiurgic process. We

don't judge the accuracy of the resulting construction, but rather see them as the enablers of collective story-telling.

These constructed 'future worlds' then serve as a canvas for creating new interesting concepts. They could be also used as a tool to discuss the desired (or undesired) new identities and practices (the 'future selves'), both on a personal and collective level).

Gained in many projects, our experience shows that this process of playful modelling of the future worlds results in much more diverse and nuanced ideas about the possible futures, or in Future Complex in our terminology.

Needless to say, the very fact that participants need to build these worlds (especially if this happens during the workshops, and their kits include all sorts of toys, trifles and trinkets) creates certain resistance itself. Our experience shows that these temporary, situational resistances are relatively easy to overcome using various workshop facilitation techniques.

What is essential is that such practice of creation of the future worlds — and especially if it is done by several groups simultaneously who would later collide and confront their creations with each other — helps to disrupt our existing inertias and to develop more complex representations of the possible futures.

Reflections on playful interventions and resistance

There are a couple of important moments that should be mentioned here. No tricks and tools can save the 'serious game' that does not fit a specific situation. When we develop our games and playful interventions, we regularly customize them, taking into account specifics of certain clients and contexts. Applications of these playful interventions depend on the client's previous experiences, their general attitude to 'gamification' as well as their general readiness for — or resistances to — the changes.

Before we develop our 'serious games' or decide which format of playful intervention would be appropriate, we run multiple 'diagnostic' procedures and evaluate various aspects that will define the final 'gameplay'. In other words, our 'counter-resistance' is preemptive, as we already try to anticipate what kind of reaction will be caused by a particular game in case of this or that client.

The dramatic and painful developments of Covid-19 that shocked the world in 2020 necessitate us to reflect on our 'playful' approach and re-evaluate its appropriateness and effectiveness.

The very first insight comes from revisiting the projects that we have conducted during a few previous years. In some of them our clients blissfully missed — or actively denied - the very opportunity of a global pandemic or similar grim developments. Yet in some other projects – and these tend to be the projects where we were truly 'playing' with the futures – such negative developments had been at least imagined and considered. We don't want to claim that we 'predicted' Covid-19 pandemics, but at least the teams who tried to imagine somewhat more complex futures, came better prepared to the developments in the year 2020.

At the same time, these very post-Covid developments continue to force us to rethink our tools and approaches, including the ones of playfulness. None of our earlier developed gameplays can be applied in this new situation as such, and this requires us to re-evaluate the current unfolding context again and again (including the appearance of very new resistances, too).

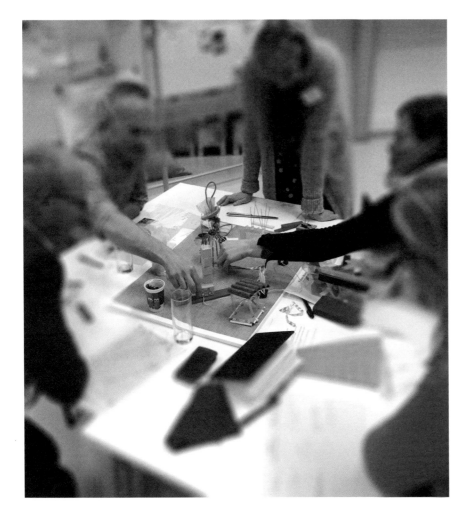

Future worlds

1

1 A poetic lens on research and creativity

Fit Associates (US)

The fast pace of work and the pressure to perform too often drives teams to move quickly through the creative process. One unfortunate result of speed is shallowness. In research, we are tempted to spend less time with the people who will be affected by our work, treating them as resources from which we extract information rather than co-creators that hold deep wells of stories and meaning. In reflection we often default to simple analysis, looking for patterns in the cold data we've collected, but not truly holding conversation with the flows of life that surround our work. In making we feel pressure to deliver, and seldom take time to put our materials and resources in extended conversation with sensed possibility.

In our experience at Fit Associates, play is one antidote to these temptations. In particular, what we might call "poetic play." It doesn't have to take a long time to bring more depth to the work, and depth doesn't have to feel solemn or serious. Play brings a deeper human connection to the challenge and the work, an opening for more purposeful and profound consideration during design, and more friendship and joy of work for all involved. We sometimes involve our team, clients, and the community of use in activities like:

- Making abstract models of the challenge or situation as though looking down from high above
- Sketching ripple effects—our work will affect these people doing these activities in these places, which will affect more people in more activities in more places, which will affect...
- Writing, drawing, or even role- playing based on poetic or mythic views of what's going on and what's possible: hero's journey, inner lizards, angels and demons,...
- Inviting people to take walks in pairs or threes, preferably in nature, with two or three big questions to consider in conversation as they stroll; then gathering in a larger group to discuss themes that arose as they talked.

2

2 Recovering sandbox time

Fit Associates (US)

For us at Fit Associates, what started as an experiment has become an enduring weekly ritual. In conversation with other busy entrepreneurs, we lamented the loss of time for simple play. Our work is creative and satisfying, but always full of expectations. "How long has it been," we wondered, "since we played like kids in a sandbox, where there is no expectation that we will produce anything or perform well; we just play?"The experiment was to set aside 90 minutes together on Zoom with our friends in Mexico and Colorado. It begins with the question, "What are you thinking of doing today?" and ends with a few minutes to share what happened. Sometimes we play together, sometimes on our own. Sometimes people have a desire:

"I'm going to write," "I'm going to paint." But often we just don't know! A breakthrough "method" is this: "I'm going to lie on my back, possibly nap, until I have an idea I'm excited about. Then I'll get up and play with it." Now

a year and a half later, we've had long-distance rapid-fire photo walks together, we've written poems and essays, painted, danced our questions and our moods, napped, shared three-minute sketch challenges, improvised, and thoroughly charmed and surprised ourselves with what can happen in 90 minutes of open play. Through it all we are recovering lost wisdom: open play is a key to creative depth.

3 Tools to provoke conversations

IDSL (France)

AnDi by IDSL: AnDi is the new clay to play with to design the digital world. A codeless solution to empower teams to create complex interactive experiences, multiple-displays HMIs, IoT, robotics, multisensorial experiences (visual, audio, olfactory etc), 5G, phygital, etc. Making prototypes helps teams to generate, test and pitch ideas and build bridges between people from different backgrounds.

3

Game card « A thousand disagreements don't make a conflict », imagined and designed for a French think tank on trust in society. 7 Themes (Governments and citizens. Culture and education. Finance and economic development; Management and social dialogue. Security and justice policy. Science and progress. Taboos.) 45 cards to play different points of view, exercise your sense of empathy and learn how to debate.

4 Communicating Effectively as Designers: Facts vs. Opinions

Somia CX (Indonesia & Singapore)

Client: "I don't like this."
Designer (Silent screaming: Whaaat the .....): "But this was designed according to the brief."
Client: "This isn't what I want."
Designer: "Oh... all I did was follow the brief correctly."
Client: "Change it."

Designer: Racing in my mind: I want to pull my hair and scratch your face.

This is such a common conversation, but of course, exists in different forms. Communication has always been an area of interest for me, personally. I have not studied it deeply but of late, the topic has come up in many ways in different contexts and I thought I'd share what I have learned recently.

The following are quick tips on how we can communicate more effectively:

Differentiate – With every conversation, make it a practice to differentiate Assertions from Assessments. Assertions are facts, nothing we can change about them. Assessments are opinions, they are NOT the truth. You will get better over time!

Grounding assessments – Now that you have acquired this new distinction, you then have a choice to 'ground' the assessment. If you receive an assessment, for e.g. Person A who happens to have no aesthetics sense (Note that this is an assessment! But it could be from your previous experience with Person A that you derive this assessment.), gives you feedback that the design is not pleasant-looking, you may choose to ignore

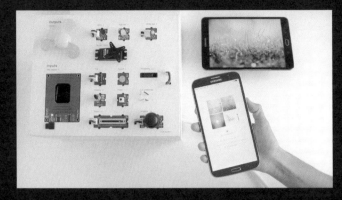

3

4

that comment and not do anything about it, versus a fellow designer who gives you similar feedback, you can then find out further what ought to be changed.

Care — Lastly, whether you are serving up your assessment to others or someone giving you their opinion, know that they have an impact and that we take more care with giving and receiving them. Human relationships are highly complex and precious. It is our responsibility to care for every conversation we make.

5 Implicit and explicit practices

Apogee (Hong Kong)

The work environment affects the person's growth and development — as well as the person's behavior, body, mind. and heart. What people do or do not do and how they behave within an environment has a very big impact on others. There are implicit and explicit behavioral practices at play — such as muscle memory —

of which many people are not usually aware. People often absorb such implicit practices unintentionally because of their cultural background, habits, personality, education, and family contexts. By giving greater exposure to these implicit practices through the use of a tool such as practice spotting and helping people learn how to spot and practice them, we hope that people will become more aware of when their own and others' implicit practices are at play.

Consider the microinteractions and behaviors in the moments between people and the impact they have on you and the people around you. These microinteractions and behaviors include words and actions—examples include taking time to listen, say thank you, or offer the courtesy of allowing another person to go first.

The appetite for meaning at work recognizes that the essence of work is increasingly used to produce knowledge. Either instead of producing things — or in addition to producing them. By introducing a renewed focus on meaning, one considers the why of work, rather than simply the what.

People develop 'character' from self reflection. And because they never work alone, reflective conversations about the ways of work can replace rote patterns of behavior with awareness. One surprising dynamic occurs at the practical boundary between rote behaviors and our more contemplative ones. Particularly, how people enter into the psychological space of a workshop and what they might leave behind as they return to the space called 'business as usual'.

This section offers ways of re-humanizing organisations for meaningful and caring outcomes. Practices that positively impact culture and bridge the gap between how people feel and how they could feel at work.

Reflective Practices for Meaningful Cultures

Daniel Szuc & Jo Wong (Apogee, Hong Kong), Lekshmy Parameswaran & Laszlo Herczeg (The Care Lab, Spain) and Nicolas Gaudron & Virginia Cruz (IDSL, France)

In most organizations today cultures are primarily about transactions and delivery, which is very challenging and stressful for people. Such workplaces and cultures do not encourage explicit moments to stop, reflect, share stories, practice and learn. This leads to unhealthy and sometimes toxic and uncaring cultures.

When there is a gap between how good people feel and how good they could feel—that is, when work cultures are not as meaningful as it could be, quality suffers. Encouraging behaviours that make meaningful and caring culture requires the creation of spaces and environments to motivate people to take responsibility to insert meaning and to build, strengthen and deepen healthy relationships and healthy behaviours.

Using the Practice Spotting tool, as developed by Apogee, we observe, identify, and make sense of stories in cultures to discover the practices implicit in the stories, so you can make them explicit, and reveal behaviors that contribute to healthy cultures for individuals and teams.

By increasing people's conscious exposure to practices and giving them tools they need to help them spot these practices in stories, as well as spaces within which to practice them, we hope people will become more aware of their own practices, make them more explicit, and encourage positive environments and behaviors within these practices.

By introducing a renewed focus on meaning and care in cultures to practice spot and create reflective practices in cultures, we close the gap and in consideration of the why of work, rather than simply the what.

Meaningful work and cultures

Some people have never experienced working on a healthy, well-functioning team so they don't know how it feels to work within such a culture. They might never have experienced a supportive, caring, pleasant culture at work.

Culture is a frequently used term to describe the behavioural happenings in organisations. For some of us we are outsiders invited in to observe organisational culture and for some of us we are insiders who work in organisations and experience the culture daily in some shape or form. Anyone can be influenced by a culture based on our interactions with it.

The challenge is we never get to fully get to understand cultures as they are constantly in flux due to the movements of people, time, place and practices at play. But it lends a question in who is responsible for explicitly being leaders of cultures to ensure that people are not only doing their transactional work outputs but also looking after the meaningful outcomes in the nurturing of the cultures people work in.

When people don't feel good about some or all of these things, their work is not meaningful to them. Or not as meaningful as it could be. People may or may not consciously dwell upon these individual elements of work. Plus, the way they're feeling frequently changes based on whatever is going on inside them—internal things—and whatever is going on outside of them—external things.

Whether we look at these things collectively or individually, when there is a gap between how good people feel and how good they could feel—that is, when work is not as meaningful as it could be—that is when its quality suffers. Their work feels like a waste of time and energy. They're on a frantic treadmill and have no real purpose. As a consequence, people experiencing unnecessary stress become demotivated, disengaged, numb, and are just biding their time—or worse exist in an unhealthy environment.

Unfortunately, there is typically little time for being in learning mode within work contexts, whether for individuals or teams. Often, organizations fail to invest in the creation of learning environments, but somehow expect people to improve magically and gain deeper practices over time.

Reflective Practices

Our observations of cultures have revealed behaviors that demonstrate a hyper focus on process, methods, deliverables, and measures—and the expectation is that people work at light speed. The language in cultures reinforces speed as the primary intention—at the expense of mindful consideration of the work and resulting in a lack of time for practice. This is a matter of grave concern.

If people are indeed too busy to think, this could cloud our vision, put blinkers on us that create tunnel vision, and obscure the more important issues at play. Issues that really matter. By slowing down, we can gain greater clarity and perspective and look further ahead.

There are some practices that are constantly in play, but are hidden from view. We call these implicit practices. They are embedded in behaviors between people that we are not always aware of or do not always pay attention to. We are unintentionally influenced by implicit practices in our own environments—comprising our cultures, habits, personality, education, family, and more.

By generating and regenerating positive practices within our environment, we can reduce intangible sources of waste—such as stress that degrades people's immune system and overall health, impacting the way they work and live.

Cultures to learn enable people to do the following

Build meaningful foundations. Focus and reflect on the practices necessary to build a foundation, including but not limited to safety, trust, authenticity, belonging, respect, and active listening. After doing this, people should feel more relaxed about making things together, independent of the quality. This should also help them to withdraw their attention from the transactional part of making meaningful work together and focus on the meaning they can glean from the experience.

Foster meaningful and caring cultures. Next, turn your attention toward both the roles and the content. Give people an opportunity to swap their roles to let people look at roles from various perspectives.

Sustain meaningful and caring cultures. The consistent repeatability of good practices is essential. Journals can help people continue to use, refer to, and record thoughts. They may sketch their observations, use key reflection moments for deeper dives into the practices that are relevant to making meaningful, and discover contextual practices for the group they're working with.

Lenses

As you go into a culture having an explicit understanding of your own lenses is critical in enabling deeper and more reflective conversations. The practice of reflection can afford us moments that encourage the practice of curiosity, prompting new thinking right now and informing a healthier future. Encouraging workplaces to take enough time for reflection and pursuing ideas or practices that pique their curiosity and in consideration of the following meta lenses:

1 **Attitude + mindset** — open or closed
2 **Perspectives + opportunities** — past, present, and future
3 **Communication + intent** — individual and team outcomes
4 **Impact + time** — success based on commitment

These meta lenses help to more explicitly understand, sense and spot the practices within the interactions and relationships, as well as the care, respect, goodwill, and good energies they demonstrated or lack of these.

Using our lenses we also create scaffolding in the form of five elements:

Cultural Leader
Understanding cultures implies being aware and playing an active role in influencing the cultures we interact with on a routine basis. We believe this is as equally a critical role for a person to play as actually doing the work of making itself on a product or service for an organisation.

Trust and Safety Between People
Understanding cultures means understanding people so taking the time to chat with people is a good place to start. Depending on your relationship with the people, time and place you need to create a sense of trust and safety between yourself and the people you are getting to know. You also want to get an idea of what problems people face in the current environment and what matters to them going forward.

Performance versus Potential
In understanding organisations it is common to focus on the perform- ance of roles in what they do in the transactions of their work and the outputs or deliverables they create. This is often described as key performance indicators to measure a productivity of sorts. We suggest part of this language in the perform- ance part of the heart is borrowed from the industrial age ways of working and can lean towards dehumanizing people in the work they do.

It can also create nasty situations where people are gaming their numbers as they compete with others that encourages unhealthy cultures and in some cases goes against the merits of the performance based system to begin with. We choose not to focus on performance but also not to ignore it. Rather we choose to focus on potential.

Learning Communities Energise Culture
One of the greatest flaws in organisational design are departments. Departments can disconnect people from other departments and fracture or disconnect a sense of community inside organisations and shut people off from outside perspectives. This results in a lack of care, compassion, empathy and even more problematically shared practice across departments causing false assumptions about other departmental cultures that may get in the way of making meaningful outcomes together.

Learning Communities are a lovely way to get people to meet up, relate and connect with the help of project stories to gain a sense of a shared culture.

Practice Card Library
We have noticed that, in the midst of project work, there is typically little time for people to practice. Plus, people from various backgrounds and functions sometimes lack the intent to work meaningfully together.

Working meaningfully together online brings even more challenges. The Covid-19 crisis has shown the importance of creating online caring cultures and environments. What we have seen during this global pandemic is that due to the use of remote collaborative software the stress of people has increased.

In order to work remotely, people exclusively use digital tools to access and provide information, follow- up on project progress, reporting, communication, book virtual meeting rooms, and maintain working relationships. These digital tools are not designed to leave blank space, play, experimentation, self expression, or creativity, They are built for efficiency, productivity, and speed.

The challenge is to find room for creativity within the use of these digital tools for taking time, slowing down, emptiness and blurriness that are at the core of creativity, and play. If not, it is difficult to allow a caring culture to sustain and foster. At IDSL, we spotted this already prior to the pandemic in various design teams.

Design tools that have been designed for fast delivery have pervaded design practices. They are easy to use and designed for quick delivery of results, by providing libraries for ready assets. By pervading design work, creativity, experimentation have shrunk or fought to exist, specifically on projects that include digital systems, interfaces and hardware that are quite complex to design and prototype.

This shows the importance of practices to create meaningful working cultures in order to build a resilient group of people who can find solutions and adapt to unknown situations where current processes are not applicable any longer, like we have seen with the COVID crisis.

Be intentional in creating environments and practice moments for meaningful and caring cultures. These could be as informal as a conversation over lunch. However, for people to improve, you really need deeper reflection and a more sustained environment for practice spotting, writing practice cards, creating a practice card library, and encouraging moments for practice.

Example Practice Card

Title
Respect

Description
Feelings of deep admiration for someone or something that are elicited by their abilities, qualities, or achievements and are influenced by your beliefs or experiences.

Benefits
Seeing others' points of view
Expanding your own view of the world
Creating questions that enhance curiosity
Seeing things you may not have seen before

Activities
Speak to someone from a group you know nothing about
Try a food you've never tried before
Watch a foreign film

Related Practices
Boundary Setting

Calls to Action

In order to effectively re-humanize organisations for meaningful and caring outcomes that can be measured for deeper sustained impact over time, we should move from focusing only on the transactional nature of the delivery of outputs using process, and moving towards the meaningful nature of outcomes using practices that positively impact on culture. In addition, we should take responsibility for our own practices where we should all play an even more explicit role through the use of values to drive practices to behavioural outcomes in caring cultures.

Spend an hour each day examining the potential for a project's significance through practice spotting by following these essential practices:

- Be caring, compassionate, and flexible and connect the dots

- Do not fall into the trap of thinking in absolutes

- Be a curious, generous, life-long learner

- Evolve your perspectives, locally and globally, to enhance diversity and think beyond the status quo

- Welcome all disciplines to create a broader community of aspiration.

1 Why Make Meaningful Work, medium.com/make-meaningful-work/why-4cba31945f63

2 Sparkle Studio and the Make Meaningful Work Show, www.uxmatters.com/mt/archives/2019/09/sparkle-studio-and-the-make-meaningful-work-show.php

3 The Emerging Economic Renaissance, www.academyforchange.org/2020/05/11/emerging-economic-renaissance/

4 Listen with your heart 用心聆聽 with Jo Wong, medium.com/make-meaningful-work/listen-with-your-heart-%E7%94%A8%E5%BF%83%E8%81%86%E8%81%BD-78d7e58c4deb

5 5 Signs Of High Emotional Intelligence, www.spring.org.uk/2020/06/5-signs-of-high-emotional-intelligence.php

6 Catalyze experimentation in design, medium.com/idsl/catalyze-experimentation-in-design-6aa9c572281c

1

1 Dr. Sparkle Toolkit

The Care Lab (Spain)

"If I have to be more time with a patient I do it, but then I suffer because I worry that the others have to wait. I complain many times about the time per patient but they see it and do not fix it anyway." Resigned Doctor

2 Taking time for interaction

Apogee (Hong Kong)

You should understand and define the problem you're solving before proposing solutions. In defining intentions, team members should take the time to interact with one another and their stakeholders, sharing existing knowledge. Develop a plan and agree upon your project's focus, exploring how this will determine the quality of project outcomes.

3

3 Future Workspaces

STBY (Netherlands & UK)

In 2018 STBY was asked to conduct an exploratory study for enterprises who were pioneering with smart office spaces to better accommodate the need for flexible teamwork. The study revealed a strong need for spaces that enable team collaboration and social interaction, in addition to open plan offices with hot desks. Interestingly, when we carried out a similar study during the pandemic in 2020, this time on 'Hybrid Working' (where people split their time between working from home and in-office), we found similar needs for online working spaces. In the past year, many enterprise workers have had a taste of working-from-home. and many are considering this to be a part of their post-COVID working pattern, but they still crave suitable spaces for creative collaboration and social interaction. And their digital tools need to cater for that.

Alongside remote-working software, such as Google Workspace, Microsoft Teams, Zoom, Slack and Dropbox, people have experimented with digital whiteboards, virtual co-working spaces, and online social game environments. They have tried to integrate these into their new hybrid working routines. Meanwhile, people also experienced frustration, in particular around creative collaborative teamwork and maintaining their social relationship with co-workers. No matter if it's in a physical space or a virtual space, large enterprises around the world have to carefully consider how to better support creativity and connections between team workers.

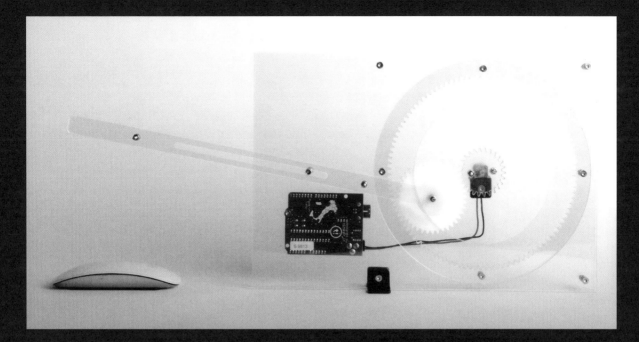

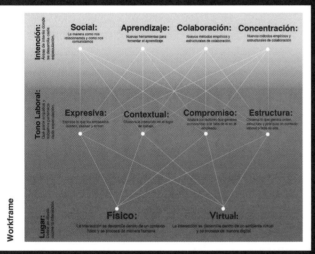

4 Office Futures Project

delaO design studio (Mexico)

Office Futures is a platform created by Jorge
Diego Etienne and José de la O for future
speculation about the office space through
research and critical design. By visiting
current open office environments, looking at
technological trends, interviewing several
stakeholders in the field and lots of research,
delaO design studio generated a number of
forecasts that could work as a starting point to
generate different design briefs. This platform
shares research and tools for speculative
projects, as well as designed briefs for new
projects, workshops and contests. This generates
a vision of the office space futures and gives
us the opportunity to understand it in order
to overcome the challenges that arise with new
realities.

Connect

While centralisation has long been the dominant frame for innovation, design, and policy, a more decentralised local reframing nowadays gains ground. The 'local' in this section points to an increasing need to take *place* and *locality* into account. Especially important as we are shifting (back) from putting economic growth in the centre of innovation and production towards putting humans, nature and the planet in the centre.

The four examples shared by the authors show how the new or returned 'local' leads to decentralised resilience in India and the Danish island of Samsø. The examples illustrate how decentralised resilience,

deep contextual knowledge, and local sustainable innovation can guide our actions in the future. The island of Samsø for example, is now a climate leader, and is awarded as an example of transformational and replicable government action at a national, regional and community level.

The authors help us to understand the momentum for the 'return of the local' better, and help us realise that local sustainable knowledge about food production, biodiversity, and forest ecosystems might play a key role in facing the challenges of the most recent period in earth's history: The Anthropocene.

The return of the local

Tipping the center-periphery balance through a re-emergence of local production and place-based communities in a globalised world

Babitha George & Romit Ray (Quicksand, India) and Rikke Ulk (Antropologerne, Denmark)

Thinking about the 'local' in light of COVID-19, points to local as something not opposed to global, but to local as something alive, taking place and happening: 'Life'. Life is happening with and among life forms in very many specific places, on interconnected, interdependent, distinct and different locations on the surface of the Earth. Every day. How people around the surface of the Earth produce food, how they collaborate, exchange goods, stories, ideas; how they impact, depend on, exploit or co-exists with their natural surroundings and how they develop material and digital infrastructures has suddenly been revealed to us during the pandemic.

Thinking about the 'local' touches on at least three important perception models:

First, we currently live in an anthropocene epoch of our planet Earth, the Age of Man. Meaning: "a period of time during which human activities have impacted the environment enough to constitute a distinct geological change" (Lynn Margulis). Our planet is inherently affected by Human life.

Second, our current production forms and life forms seem to cherish and need depth, belonging and redundancy (strong, 'thick' and 'local' systems are more difficult to threaten, as opposed to fragile, optimized and globalized systems that more easily fall apart, for instance when politics

and the specialized supply chain are challenged).

Thirdly, we witness many examples of how people in communities all around, in rural areas as well as in communities and neighbourhoods in big cities, are deliberately building up resilience by reinforcing local infrastructure, inventing and reinventing local food production, farming, new forms of belonging and experiencing roots and resilience within a place.

The idea of *decentralisation* or *deglobalisation* and what it means to be 'local', redundant and resilient today is calling for attention, as an alternative to centralised organisational forms in the current disrupted global system. The highly specialised interconnected global production system has been long touted as the panacea for many of the challenges faced by humankind. But it is fragile and vulnerable when met by a global pandemic. And it has for long been fragile, dressed up as hard, and vulnerable, dressed up as powerful, not taking into account and considering nature, natural resources, animal life, trees, plants, climate and the well-being of the planet.

While *centralisation* long has been the dominant frame for innovation, design, policy, etc., nowadays the 'local' points to a more prominent need to take 'place' and locality into account. The global, centralized system has for long not been proven to offer much value for smaller communities, as we can read in the Indian examples in this essay. And if we look at contextual or place based innovation, it is a kind of innovation that emerges out of and in response to a sense of place, and to sharing *purpose* in smaller communities, as illustrated in the Danish example. In the new or returned local we can find multiple examples of how it leads to decentralised *resilience*, a concept and model worth looking into as we move ahead in the new era.

Below four examples that may help us understand a return of the 'local' better:

Decentralised resilience

Farming in rural contexts in India often involves a significant amount of trial and error to mitigate the impact of ever-changing weather patterns and market demands. This practice requires a dynamism and adaptability on the part of the farmers that is often constrained by well-intended but stringent policies. In an effort to enforce quality standards compliance and integration with existing infrastructure, government involvement can easily have a restrictive effect on farmers' livelihoods. How can new affordances be created in the relationship between local communities and legislators, that takes the local into account more strongly?

An experienced farmer belonging to a group with solid farming credentials — had taken to doing odd jobs and even contemplated suicide. Then he realised

that the raw sewage that passed by his farmland could change his fortunes. He started using raw sewage to irrigate his land and growing mulberry, which is fodder for silkworms and is not consumed directly by humans, thereby mitigating adverse effects of raw sewage. He asks the question — should he pay the town for using the sewage, or should the town pay him for treating its sewage? Lack of empirical data is used to discredit new approaches, raising questions of how much policy-making relies on data collection technology. Stories of conservation are always questioned and the lack of data behind the stories raises questions of equity, transparency and representation. In addition, the government technology infrastructure is very different from the tech infrastructure that communities/ locals put up themselves; their objectives are also very different: big data allows the government to make claims and gives them leverage. Additionally, data becomes about vouching for an idea and reduces accountability and the inherent quality of the idea.

How might local knowledge be recognised and integrated into the local implementations of state-wide policies?

How might a safe space (financial or technical) be created for experimentation to thrive and mature?

How might farmers build on each others' knowledge to consolidate their respective findings and gain a stronger voice in policy discussions?

How might policy makers be inspired by local ingenuity and inventivity?

How might local farmers be incentivised to share the knowledge they develop? How might it be made mutually beneficial in farmer communities and when interacting with policy makers?

How might rituals that connect us to our past be reimagined in new forms, while respecting and acknowledging their roots?

Deep contextual knowledge

Biodiversity is often studied and calculated in a scientifically prescribed manner. Biodiversity hotspots and forest

areas across India are often inhabited by indigenious populations who have a deep and nuanced understanding of the forest ecosystem. These communities may have their own methodologies to assess biodiversity, which even though not scientific, are highly suited to the specific geographies and ecologies that they call home. How can traditional knowledge be combined with scientific approaches to imagine new innovative and highly contextual ways of not only measuring but also preserving and regenerating biodiversity?

The Soligas (indigenous people in the BR Hills area in Karnataka in India) have an intuitive understanding of forest ecosystems. This is different from a lot of us, who become aware of these things only as a result of ecological education. This was evident when a Soliga man told us about how lantana (originally planted by the British as a decorative plant, but has now taken over the forest) is leading to a loss of mobility and grazing grounds for deer, which are reducing in number and which in turn is reducing tiger populations in the forest. They see the forest ecology as a finely balanced harmonious thing, which can be destroyed by forces from the outside — such as the lantana.

Tree cover or shade is often measured with a densiometer and if the reading is high, one may be quick to conclude that the forest is healthy. However, a densiometer does not take care of biodiversity — as all the trees could be the same species (such as silver oak) and that is not healthy. The more manual and sensory evaluation of biodiversity of the Soliga seems to be better suited than just a densiometer, which may be accurate but does not serve the purpose.

The Soliga have over the years been forced by the government out of the forest and this continues today. Younger members of the Soliga community are becoming detached from the forest, forgetting songs, tales and forest paths. The older members of the community find this tragic.

The Soliga language, which is also being lost, is unique and one can make an educated guess that it is highly attuned to that specific forest.

The Soliga community has done a commendable job of cataloguing the forest around them. But this cataloguing

Clockwise from top: Small sustainable coffee farming in BR Hills, Karnataka;
Multicropping in a small natural farm in the outskirts of Bangalore;
Fly catching contraption in a natural farm in rural Karnataka

is not for the purposes of exploitation, which is interesting as cataloguing and categorising of spaces and populations is often linked to exploitation. Instead, soligas have names for trees, shrubs, animals etc that are quite comprehensive. Furthermore, they remember these names and recognise these species. This is usually seen only among seasoned biologists and zooligists, who unlike the Soligas are specialists and have a narrow focus. However, the focus of the Soligas is the entire forest ecosystem.

How can this vibrant sense of place and the resulting practices not be systematically invalidated? Instead, how can we build on and center this nuanced, deep and unconventional understanding that indigenous communities bring to vital issues such as biodiversity and conservation?

Local sustainable innovation

Scale is a crucial factor in evaluating ideas around innovation, entrepreneurship and policy making. However, scaling ideas and solutions often disregard local knowledge, constraints, ecologies and traditions. Furthermore, because only scalable ideas find any kind of traction, more local and contextualised innovations find little support, as has been the case in India for long. Sustainable and ecological innovation requires localized approaches that are tailored to meet the requirements of local ecologies. Often, only local innovations can respond to the specific challenges and needs of contexts. How can we articulate counter narratives to scale that evaluate ideas not on their ability to scale, but instead, their ability to remain local and contextual? Such perspectives and evaluative approaches can lead to new funding models that are more eco-friendly and sustainable.

The 'Green Revolution' was the ultimate scale oriented model that transformed India's agriculture. However, the insistence on standardisation and best practices meant that the same techniques, thought processes and philosophies

were applied in all ecologies and climates in India. Over decades this has led to severe soil quality deterioration. The government machinery driving the Green Revolution ensured that local ideas and practices were ignored and in many cases lost. Because agriculture is not simply an occupation but a way of living and organising societies, change in agricultural practices often means changes in social structures.

'Self-Limiting geographies' can emerge as a key attribute to judge ideas by. In many ways this is the opposite of scale as it judges ideas based on their ability to contain themselves in geographies that are conducive to them. What is important to realise, articulate and promote are the kinds of processes that generate ideas that are self-limiting. In fact rooted communities may naturally gravitate towards thinking that is self-limiting. Scale on the other hand is perhaps more an emergent phenomenon being fueled by globalization and modern business practices. Recording of local biocultural protocols can support self-limiting and contextual innovations and practices. (once you know what is the local biocultural tradition, you have a better sense of what is good locally and what is not). Bio-regions as concepts can also lead to more sustainable solutions. Bio-regions combine the idea of self-limiting geographies with a biocultural approach. What you get are ideas, systems, innovations etc that are limited to certain bio-regions.

A sense of place and a consideration of here will guide our actions in the future

'Ø' is the Danish word for Island. And the name of the island Samsø (a small island in the middle of Denmark) means gathering, meeting up, being together. The naming goes back to when the Vikings would meet at the 'little gathering island in the middle' before raging and plundering the Englishmen and communities further

away. However, nowadays Samsø is better known as 'Renewable Energy Island of Denmark'. And since October 6th 2021 as 'Climate Leader' according to the United Nations Climate Action Award. For the first, but hopefully not the last time in history, a local community is chosen as an example of important climate action. Inspired by a competition in 1997, initiated by visionary Minister of Environment from the Danish government Svend Auken, people and politicians from the local community of Samsø got together, established the Energy Academy of Samsø and invested in windmills. They changed and owned their own energy-supply-chain, and in doing so they made an effort that is scalable and replicable. The case of Samsø showed how to replace oil and fossil energy sources with green energy supplies from locally and democratically owned and built windmills on land and in the sea. Samsø is now a Climate Leader, together with the City of Paris in France and 'Metropolitan area of Guadalajara' in Mexico (2021). All three were awarded as examples of transformational and replicable government action at a national, regional and community level.

Samsø was 100% self-sufficient with renewable energy in 2007, and is now working towards being 100% fossil free in 2030. One driver for the local community of 3.700 islanders and the municipality of Samsø was to create a demonstration of how to diminish the negative impact on the climate, the planet and the land. Other equally, and for some even more, important drivers were the infrastructural and societal changes made, which entailed creating employment and securing continuous settlement and survival of the small population. This fostered resilience and a local identity of being on a quest together. The Samsø example beautifully shows how self-interest walks hand in hand with large-scale ideological interest. The mobilization of local shareholders in the new, daring, windmill project gave a sense of common ground and purpose to the islanders. In an analysis of the participation and engagement of the islanders in the energy island-project (2014, by Antropologerne) the concept 'HERE' was expressed as special and spatial for the Samsø-identity. When talking about the energy island project the word 'HERE' used by the locals refers to *place* (as in *here* on Samsø) but also to *purpose* or *cause* (as in this thing here, that we are up to). In 2018 Rikke Ulk, co-author of this essay, moved to Samsø with her family and company, and is now participating in the development of new sustainable initiatives on the island.

In the public debate in Denmark and in places such as The World Economic Forum in Davos (2020) we see a shift from only putting economic growth in the centre of innovation and production towards instead putting humans, nature and the planet in the center of how we innovate, produce our food and organize our lives. A much broader definition of value than money, based on empathy and a deep realisation of connectedness seems to be more and more highly rated. The plain economic reasoning is losing power as the motivation for and the driver of change. Circular business models are combined with traditional and new local knowledge and skills. And in a country like Denmark, and on Samsø, this is also often fueled by digital production technologies (*open source*, 3D print, new funding infrastructure and new social media

launches) that re-center and give birth to a more green and more local production in both big city communities and small village societies.

Today, after more than 20 years as 'Renewable Energy Island', Samsø is also redefining sustainability in other aspects of local life than energy and community power. The garden of Ydun (#ydunshavev, a small ecological farm) is one example. It is run by a family who do not own the farm but take care of it and operate it. A CSA, a community supported agriculture-business model with local 'members' meeting up every Thursday to fetch the vegetables, herbs and fruits of the week, secure sales and support the farm. A bigger stakeholder-community owns the farm (and other farms) and leases it to young newly educated farmers. Small food brands like #ølaks (locally smoked salmon), #samsølam (traditional sheep meat and sausages) #linserforlivet (lentils for life, Samsø lentils), and #samsømel (flour) are other examples of products being produced ecologically and locally. And also new sustainable businesses like #øbo, sustainable shops like #øro and #samsømicrobrewery, and a sustainable school (the school in the forest) are being realized at Samsø.

Conclusion

At some point civilisation agreed that there was a great interest in moving from 'local' to 'global' — from an archaic past to a modern and globalised present and future. For many years global and globalization were associated with increasing diversity. But nowadays global is more accurately understood as a provincial extension of what it means to live in the globalized world, where 'global' and 'globalization' is eating up the diversity of lifeforms. This is the argument of the French philosopher, anthropologist and sociologist Bruno Latour in a video lecture on the Anthropocene (18 June 2018). Our resolution should not be: 'let's go back to the local'. Let's not return to the old 'local' as opposed to 'global'. Latour puts an emphasis on the place and surface of the earth: The soil, the surface, we see and live upon when we inhabit and live on this planet.

In our words this 'place' of belonging is resilient here. Both local and global, but foremost a special and spatial place on this earth, that we should and will try to balance and take care of.

Views of children playing and the vegetable garden at the Forest School on the island of Samsø, Denmark

1

1 We are not from Mars, we are from Africa

STBY (Netherlands & UK), Matchboxology (South Africa)

As Spotify was planning to expand to Eastern and Western Africa, they realised they needed to strengthen their connections to local music cultures. Not just for the music, but also for their visual cultures. Matchboxology and STBY ran a series of online co-creative workshops with people from the music industry and graphic designers in Kenya, Tanzania, Uganda, Nigeria and Ghana. This was during the pandemic, so everything was done online. Participants collected images that could represent the music cultures in their countries. They also suggested a range of African image makers who could become suppliers to Spotify for its visual playlist covers. One of the results of the project was a poster with instagram images from key African image makers and their contact details, to inspire the Spotify design team and allow them to make easy connections.

2 Trust in Science project

STBY (Netherlands & UK), delaO design studio (Mexico), Flutter Innovation (Brazil), Matchboxology (South Africa), Quicksand (India)

The Reach Network completed two projects for Wellcome Trust that helped the organisation with a strategic review during the pandemic and provide effective medical and science support in developing countries around the world. The first project drew lessons from Zika, Ebola and Covid-19, and focused on vulnerable groups in 5 countries and key players who build (or damage) these groups' trust in health science. The second project put together a landscape analysis across 4 regional areas and captured a picture of how young people are involved in the 3 priority areas for Wellcome: Infectious, Disease, Mental Health and Climate & Human Health.

Though both studies were desk research, the benefit of having local partners is obvious. Each

2

4

partner involved in the study was able to quickly target the relevant information source in the local area, analyse non-English data and provide contextual interpretation for news, articles and academic papers. This collaboration allowed us to quickly identify what were cross-location patterns and what's unique to certain local areas due to its cultural and historical contexts.

3 Zooming in and zooming out

Apogee (Hong Kong)

We need to gain perspectives that let us see more widely and deeply by: Listening to other people's perspectives; Probing to see what we may not immediately see; Zooming out to gain greater perspective; Zooming in on the details within the bigger picture. Then, we must share and clarify our perspectives by: Confronting the issues to help solve problems; Connecting the dots to gain

focus. Finally, we need to define meaning (based on our perspectives) by: Knowing what we need to work on and why; Prioritizing what work to focus on now; Focusing on that work and its meaning.

4 Coping with the pandemic

delaO design studio, Mexico

Desde Casa is a journalistic exercise we began as a response to the COVID-19 pandemic. Through this platform we discussed and reflected on our daily challenges as Mexicans, but also as designers. Through research, writing, interviews, design briefs and different types of content, we tried to bring feasible solutions that people can use to cope with the pandemic and led the attention to those new challenges that we had to face since 2020.

Reach

About the Reach Network

Love Local, Reach Global
Reach is a global network of agencies specialised in human-centred design research and service innovation, working with businesses and non-profit organisations around the world. Some of the clients and partner organisations we work with are seeking to improve existing services, or to develop new offerings in multiple international markets.

World-wide network of design research specialists
As a network organisation, we conduct design research, training and coaching for distributed teams at a local level, while maintaining a global vision. In bespoke combinations Reach partners closely collaborate on international projects for client organisations. We also co-produce publications, local meet-ups and international events that celebrate the results of these partnerships and share learnings.

Training and coaching via the Reach School
Our international training and coaching programmes support organisations with strengthening their internal capacity. We offer two programmes tailored to multinational corporations and non-government organisations seeking to embed sustainable and locally sensitive design driven innovation in the organisation. Co-orchestrated by Reach partners around the world, the Reach School goes beyond basic introductions to discovery research and design thinking. We combine the training sessions with coaching on actual projects.

Knowledge exchange with wider community
As experts in human-centered design and pioneers in design-driven innovation, all partners in Reach are keen to share and develop their knowledge and celebrate achievements. Together, we have hosted a number of international conferences, and several Reach partners also host their own regional conferences. Whenever possible, we try to collectively reflect on our practice and share our thoughts through various publications and articles.

Reach Network

Denmark Antropologerne
antropologerne.com

United Kingdom & Netherlands STBY
stby.eu

Russia & Netherlands Summ()n
summon-futures.com

Germany Minds & Makers
minds-makers.com

France IDSL
id-sl.com

Spain & Hungary The Care Lab
thecarelab.org

**South Africa, Tanzania &
Côte d'Ivoire** Matchboxology
matchboxology.com

Canada Big Human
bighumanchange.com

USA Fit Associates
fitassociates.com

Mexico delaO design studio
delao.mx

Brazil & Germany Flutter Innovation
flutter-innovation.com

Japan Re:public Inc
re-public.jp

China Apogee
apogeehk.com

India Quicksand
quicksand.co.in

Singapore SPUR
spurhauswerks.com

Indonesia & Singapore Somia CX
somiacx.com

Philippines Curiosity
curiosity.ph

Australia Paper Giant
papergiant.net

18 partners   28 locations   158 people

About the editors

STBY is a pioneering thought leader in the field of design research, and specifically when applied for meaningful and positive transformation. We are not just passengers of the projects we work on, but co-drivers of the change we envision in society and through our work. We are based in London and Amsterdam, and our interdisciplinary backgrounds as creatives and social researchers enable us to practice what we preach, and we have been doing so since as early as 2003. We generate value and impact on a wide range of levels, from strategy to roadmaps for implementation, and from creating new knowledge to socialising assets as part of transformation processes. www.stby.eu

Nina Stegeman is design researcher at STBY Amsterdam. She has a background in Journalism and Cultural Anthropology. As such, she does not view the world in black or white, right or wrong. For Nina, it is the responsibility of the researcher to show that experiences are layered, entangled, and interconnected. She loves to immerse herself in new contexts, meticulously analyse raw data, and craft compelling, nuanced stories for clients. Nina is frequently involved in societal, and sensitive research projects. At STBY she is a lead researcher for What Design Can Do challenges and involved in many community participation projects for the City of Amsterdam.

Geke van Dijk is co-founder and Strategy Director of STBY. She has a background in ethnographic research, user-centered design and service strategy. Her passion to bring people into the heart and soul innovation processes, and her strong drive to contribute to positive change in society has shaped the direction of STBY's portfolio of working on topics such as community participation, inclusivity and sustainability. Since founding STBY in 2003, Geke has been one of the early pioneers in the field of Service Design. She was the initiator of the Service Design Network Netherlands, and has been their chair for 10 years. She is also a co-founder of the REACH Network for Global Design Research. Geke frequently publishes presents and teaches on Service Innovation and Design Research. She holds a PhD in Computer Sciences from the Open University in the UK.

About the co-authors

Aditya Prakash is a design researcher at Quicksand, with a background in Economics, Philosophy, and Maths. As part of the HUM team, he enjoys creating meaningful and immersive speculative narratives of humanitarian work that convey insightful research findings, as well as provoke audiences to engage in difficult and necessary conversations about the problems of today. Together with a colleague, Rohan, he has been awarded the Next Gen Foresight Practitioners Asia Special Award in 2020.

Ayush Chauhan is one of the co-founders of Quicksand and leads the studio in new business, strategy and project management. Ayush is a strong advocate for transformative roles for design within public policy, international development, social enterprise and innovation, for which he was also granted the prestigious Yale World Fellowship in 2012. Ayush's current passion is to shape the venture design practice at Quicksand, bringing together knowledge and practices from the world of development and business to incubate startups that are impact-led and with strong design values. He also serves on the board of William J. Clinton Foundation in India.

Babitha George is a Director at Quicksand, a human-centred design studio based in India and the Co-founder and Director of UnBox Cultural Futures Society, a collective, building action at the intersection of disciplines. Some of the work she has led recently has been across the spaces of livelihoods, environment, sexual and reproductive health, public health, changing technology narratives and farming.

Bas Raijmakers is co-founder and Creative Director of STBY in London and Amsterdam since 2003. STBY is specialised in creative research for considerate transformation towards more human, just and sustainable societies. Bas has worked for clients in industry, government and the public sector for more than 25 years. He holds a PhD in Design Interactions from the Royal College of Art in London. Bas founded the global design research network Reach in 2008. More on www.stby.eu and reach-network.com.

In his first life, **Cal Bruns** spent 20 years working across 5 continents as a highly awarded creative director with global advertising agency Leo Burnett. Fifteen years ago, Cal founded Matchboxology, Africa's first Human Centred Design firm. Since then, he and his diverse team have worked across 18 countries unlocking social purpose, positive behaviour change and impact growth opportunities for leaders and development projects in public health, entrepreneurship development and environmental issues

Camila Boga is the Director of Design & Insights at Flutter Innovation. She has been delivering relevant insights and meaningful results with a firm belief in making life better through memorable experiences. Innovation and human-centred design are her areas of expertise. Over the last ten years, she has led innovation projects for clients, such as Bosch, Renault, Motorola, Telefonica, Electrolux, HSBC, Itaú and Diageo. Camila holds an MBA in Branding and in-depth training in Strategic Design Management at Central Saint Martins (London) and Parsons Schools of Design (NY).

Chris Marmo is the co-founder and CEO of Paper Giant, a strategic design consultancy based in Australia. He has a background in psychology, computer science and anthropology, and is a recovering academic. In his work at Paper Giant, he leads multi-disciplinary teams through complex research and design challenges using ethnographic and design research methods. Chris is passionate about the overlaps between people, technology and spaces, and holds a PhD in Anthropology from RMIT University in Melbourne. His thesis explored the overlaps between cultural geography and design, and as a result he can't help but frame everything as a space of some kind.

Daniel Szuc is a co-founder and principal at Apogee and co-founder of Make Meaningful Work, as well as the co-founder of UX Hong Kong. He has been involved in the UX field for over 20 years, and has been based in Hong Kong for over 20 years. Dan has lectured about user-centered design globally. He has co-authored two books including Global UX with Whitney Quesenbery and the Usability Kit with Gerry Gaffney.

José de la O is an Industrial Designer specialized in design research. He is Director of delaO design studio, his design and research agency based in Mexico City. José is currently Regional Director of the Design Department at Monterrey Institute of Technology and Higher Education in México City. José has an Industrial Design Bachelor Degree from Universidad Iberoamericana and a Masters Degree on Contextual Design from Design Academy Eindhoven, graduating in 2010. The same year, he founded de la O design studio in Eindhoven, Netherlands which was later relocated to Mexico City. During his career he has incursed in product design, speculative design and strategic design, as well as design-driven research and consultancy projects, having his work exhibited and published by several national and international platforms. De la O is co-founder of Cooperativa Panorámica,. He runs the design-driven cultural initiative The Chair that Rocks, is the creative director of his design brand delaO.shop, and co-produces the spanish-language design podcast Fuera de Contexto.

Josephine Wong is a co-founder and principal at Apogee and co-founder of Make Meaningful Work, as well as the co-founder of UX Hong Kong. Jo grew up in multicultural Hong Kong, with a Chinese-Burmese father and Chinese-Indonesian mother. She collaborates with global teams conducting research in Cantonese, Mandarin and English. Jo is passionate about the environment, political and economic systems and how we can live healthier and happier lives while not adversely impacting less fortunate people.

Katerina Khomenchuk is a co-founder and research director of Summ( )n, the Netherlands-based practice that supports companies and organizations in their strategic innovation projects. Summ( )n helps its clients in gaining in-depth understanding of people's behavior and values today, in exploring how societies and cultures are changing, and in translating these insights into tangible concepts and new propositions. Prior to Summ( )n, Katerina worked with Burson-Marsteller, global PR and communication firm, where she led social and consumer studies in Russia and Central Asian to support the development of new communication strategies. Katerina's own research interests are the new, cross-platform (digital) communication practices and tools. Deeper understanding of these emerging practices, both within organizations and in the societies and cultures at large can enable more efficient transformations of (organizational) cultures.Katerina has a degree in Psychology (Psychology of Communication) and lately studied Human-Computer Interactions.

Kelvin Kaari is an insights associate at Matchboxology, Africa's first human centered design consultancy based in Johannesburg. He supports the analysis of data across multiple project verticals, driving insights that form the foundations of impactful solutions to pressing system challenges. Kelvin holds a B.A in Public Policy & Law and French Studies from Trinity College (Hartford, CT). Outside of work, Kelvin likes to attend intimate live music/comedy events and culinary immersions.

Kleber Puchaski is the VP of Product Design at Adecco Group and founder of Flutter Innovation, a network enterprise supporting companies throughout the digital transformation journey combining rational and creative thinking. Kleber is co-founder of Reach - the Global Design Research Network. Holding over 20 years of experience, Kleber has worked on identifying consumer insights, developing products and services, branding strategies, and innovation processes for companies like Zeiss, Philips, Renault, Hyundai-Kia, Telefónica, Electrolux, HSBC, and Bosch. Kleber holds an MA in Design Strategy and Branding from Brunel University - UK and a PhD in Vehicle Design from the Royal College of Art, London.

László Herczeg is a care activist and designer who has been working in the area of health and care for more than two decades. In 2008, together with Lekshmy Parameswaran, he co-founded fuelfor, a specialist design consultancy working with a wide variety of international players within the health and care sector. In 2017 they co-founded The Care Lab (www.thecarelab.org), a collaborative platform with a transversal vision of care as an equitable, pro-active and compassionate experience that forms an integral part of everyday life, from birth to death. He holds a Master of Arts degree from the Academy of Arts and Design in Budapest, including study at the University of Arts and Design in Helsinki.

Lekshmy Parameswaran is a care activist and designer who has been working in the area of health and care for over two decades. In 2008, together with László Herczegh, she co-founded fuelfor, a specialist design consultancy working with a wide variety of international players within the health and care sector. In 2017 they co-founded The Care Lab (www. thecarelab.org), a collaborative platform that uses human-centred design practices to rethink and redesign care models and solutions for our societies and care systems. She holds a Master of Engineering degree from Cambridge University and a Master of Arts from the Royal College of Art in London.

Michael Davisburchat is the Director of Big Human. Before Big Human. Mike worked as a veteran designer and innovator for organizations around the world, including time in China and the United States. An advocate for discovering the value in eradicating stubborn social challenges, he's fascinated by seemingly impossible problems (and working out how to solve them). Recently he's enjoyed time as a member of Reach, a global design-research network made up of 20 member partners across 4 continents.

Nicolas Gaudron graduated from the Royal College of Art in London, under the tutelage of Anthony Dunne and Durrell Bishop. He joined IDEO in Palo Alto. He then moved to INRIA, the French National Institute for Research in Computer Science and Automation, as member of the HCI team led by Wendy Mackay and Michel Beaudouin-Lafon. He then worked at the Renault Direction of Industrial Design,« Prospective & Concept Car» studio before starting IDSL in 2007.

Rikke Ulk is the Founder and Director of Antropologerne, the first and female-led anthropological consultancy in Denmark and Europe (founded in 2003). Rikke did study and making field work in Rio de Janeiro, Brazil and in New York City, the United States. In 2002 she obtained master's degree in anthropology from the University of Copenhagen, Denmark. Rikke has worked actively as an anthropologist consultant for more than 18 years. She is a member of REACH Network, f-i-x. dk network, the Danish Management Society Design Denmark, and has been in the Wisdom Council of Samsø Energy Academy (2015–16) and the Jury of the Danish Design Award (2018). Now she and Antropologerne are residing on the island of Samsø, Denmark.

Romit Ray is a Principal at Quicksand, a human centred design studio based in India. His background is a hybrid between humanities (sociology) and technology. As a design researcher he conducts ethnographic, contextual research that attempts to go beyond what people say and think, into what they do, know, feel and dream, while actively including individuals and communities in framing problems and solutions through an active process of design-led co-creation.

Slava Kozlov is a co-founder and currently a director of Summ( )n, the Netherlands-based practice that supports companies and organizations in their strategic innovation projects. Summ( )n helps its clients in gaining in-depth understanding of people's behavior and values today, in exploring how societies and cultures are changing, and in translating these insights into tangible concepts and new propositions. Summ( )n also facilitates the changes, using 'serious games' and different gamification techniques to transform personal and collective behavior and mindsets.Prior to Summ( )n, Slava worked for ten years with the Strategic Innovation team of Philips Design, and before that participated in numerous consumer research and social studies, both on client and research sides. Slava has degrees in Clinical Psychology and in Sociology (Social Studies of Transitional Societies).

Virginia Cruz is the first graduate of Ecole Polytechnique (France) to also graduate from the Royal College of Art in London. She also graduated from Les Mines de Paris (France) and the Imperial College in London. Her career is at the intersection of arts, science and industry at Le Louvre, Louis Vuitton, Electrolux in Sweden, Sony R&D, Sacred World Foundation in India, France Telecom R&D, Orange and IDSL. She was also member of the French National Digital Council.

Yuki Uchida is an urban designer and collective director in Japan. She graduated from Waseda University with a bachelor degree in Architecture and she majored in Sustainable City Design at Ferrara University graduate school in Italy. In 2013, she joined as a founding member of Think/Do tank Re:public. She utilises approaches such as vision building, organisational development and community design to empower individuals and develop an innovation ecosystem for the better future with local and global partners. She was appointed as a regional revitalization evangelist by the Cabinet Office in 2017. Jury member of Good Design Award in Japan.